Cambridge Elements ≡

Elements in Decision Theory and Philosophy
edited by
Martin Peterson
Texas A&M University

OPINION POOLING

Lee Elkin
Erasmus University Rotterdam

Richard Pettigrew
University of Bristol

CAMBRIDGE
UNIVERSITY PRESS

CAMBRIDGE
UNIVERSITY PRESS

Shaftesbury Road, Cambridge CB2 8EA, United Kingdom

One Liberty Plaza, 20th Floor, New York, NY 10006, USA

477 Williamstown Road, Port Melbourne, VIC 3207, Australia

314–321, 3rd Floor, Plot 3, Splendor Forum, Jasola District Centre,
New Delhi – 110025, India

103 Penang Road, #05–06/07, Visioncrest Commercial, Singapore 238467

Cambridge University Press is part of Cambridge University Press & Assessment,
a department of the University of Cambridge.

We share the University's mission to contribute to society through the pursuit of
education, learning and research at the highest international levels of excellence.

www.cambridge.org
Information on this title: www.cambridge.org/9781009494410

DOI: 10.1017/9781009315203

First published 2024

A catalogue record for this publication is available from the British Library.

ISBN 978-1-009-49441-0 Hardback
ISBN 978-1-009-31517-3 Paperback
ISSN 2517-4827 (online)
ISSN 2517-4819 (print)

Cambridge University Press & Assessment has no responsibility for the persistence
or accuracy of URLs for external or third-party internet websites referred to in this
publication and does not guarantee that any content on such websites is, or will
remain, accurate or appropriate.

Opinion Pooling

Elements in Decision Theory and Philosophy

DOI: 10.1017/9781009315203
First published online: December 2024

Lee Elkin
Erasmus University Rotterdam

Richard Pettigrew
University of Bristol

Author for correspondence: Lee Elkin, ljelkin3@gmail.com

Abstract: Disagreement is a common feature of a social world. For various reasons, however, we sometimes need to resolve a disagreement into a single set of opinions. This can be achieved by pooling the opinions of individuals that make up the group. This Element provides an opinionated survey on some ways of pooling opinions: linear pooling, multiplicative pooling (including geometric), and pooling through imprecise probabilities. While this Element gives significant attention to the axiomatic approach in evaluating pooling strategies, it also evaluates them in terms of the epistemic and practical goals they might meet. In doing so, this Element connects opinion pooling to some philosophical problems in social epistemology and the philosophy of action, illuminating different perspectives one might take when figuring out how to pool opinions for a given purpose. This title is also available as Open Access on Cambridge Core.

Keywords: opinion pooling, group belief, disagreement, collective responsibility, collective agency

ISBNs: 9781009494410 (HB), 9781009315173 (PB), 9781009315203 (OC)
ISSNs: 2517-4827 (online), 2517-4819 (print)

Contents

1 Introduction

Epidemiologists Anya, Bon, and Carys have studied the current spread of polio in developed nations, taking into account the recent decline in vaccination rates. Despite their shared interest in predicting the status of polio in the near term, the three come up with different opinions. Anya is 20% sure polio will be eradicated by 2030, Bon is 60% sure, and Carys is 70% sure.

Disagreement like this is a common feature of a social world. For various reasons, however, we sometimes need to resolve such disagreement into a single set of opinions. Perhaps we need to present a summary of the epidemiologists' views to a policymaker to inform their decision-making. Perhaps we wish to assess the track record of their predictions across time and we do so by looking at how accurate their collective opinions have been. Perhaps we wish to update our own opinions upon learning of the disagreement within the group, which amounts to combining our opinions with theirs in some way. Perhaps we wish to aggregate the individual views in order to make a decision on behalf of the group they form or to assess whether the group, taken as an agent in its own right, is liable for a particular consequence of its collective action, as we might do if the group is the board of a company or the executive committee of a trade union, for instance.

But how should we take conflicting opinions and resolve them? How should we *pool* opinions? As we'll see, there's no one pooling strategy that works for every occasion, and so we must choose among a great variety of them before we can enjoy any epistemic or practical benefits. But determining which to choose in a given situation is no easy feat. Our objective in this Element is to provide the reader with an opinionated survey of some central strategies that have garnered attention in the philosophical literature, aiming to show how to evaluate them for a specific purpose.

Throughout, we take for granted that the opinions of individuals vary in strength and are numerically represented (think of Anya, Bon, and Carys from earlier). We'll often call such opinions "credences" and, for the most part, adopt the idealized assumption that credences are probabilistically coherent, a fundamental tenet of *Bayesian epistemology* (see, e.g., Bovens & Hartmann, 2004). While there is debate over whether belief is fundamentally a categorical or graded epistemic attitude (or both), it's reasonable to think that in a world full of uncertainties, individuals tend to have less than full belief in many propositions.[1] And since this generalizes to all individuals, it's reasonable to take

---

[1] For classical accounts of credence or partial belief, see Ramsey (1926 [1931]); de Finetti (1974). It is also worth noting at this point that the opinions we seek to pool are credences in propositions; they are not estimates of quantities more generally. For instance, we will not

the opinions of group members to be graded on many matters. Furthermore, assuming that the opinions of group members vary in strength on uncertain matters allows for richer pooling strategies that groups may choose to adopt when seeking a compromise.

As it concerns the evaluation of pooling strategies, we give significant attention to the so-called *axiomatic* approach in this Element that is quite common in computer science, economics, philosophy, and statistics.[2] Pooling axioms are desirable criteria we might want a pooling strategy to meet. Since at least the 1960s, researchers have investigated which pooling functions satisfy which axioms.[3] But these systematic analyses also highlight the sacrifices that must be made when you select an aggregation rule, since one can very rarely have it all. The details of the formal constraints and their relation to pooling strategies will occupy many of the pages to come.

But before concerning ourselves with some of the intricacies of pooling functions and their properties, we begin by taking an unconventional detour through social epistemology and the philosophy of action. As things stand, there is a gulf between the formal study of opinion pooling and the conceptual analysis of related issues concerning peer disagreement, justified group belief, and group responsibility, for example. We take the latter conceptual issues to help us evaluate pooling strategies. In other words, the formal axiomatic method is not the only way of evaluating pooling mechanisms. For this reason, we review some important accounts addressing the philosophical issues, highlighting ways that they can motivate particular pooling strategies and pooling in general. In particular, we ask which pooling strategies best serve our epistemic and practical goals: for instance, we ask what pooling strategies are optimal if our goal is to produce collective credences that are as accurate as possible; and we ask what strategies work best if we wish to use the pooled credences to guide collective actions on behalf of the group.

With any luck, the questions raised intimately relating the conceptual and formal traditions will further be pursued by others in the broader study of group agency.[4] Of course, we inevitably fall short of providing a thorough analysis

---

ask how to aggregate your estimate and my estimate of the distance from Bristol to Rotterdam directly, though we would be able to do so indirectly by first pooling our credences about the different possible distances and then taking an expectation of the distance relative to those pooled credences.

[2] Some valuable surveys of the axiomatic approach can be found in Genest & Zidek (1986) and Dietrich & List (2015).

[3] See, e.g., Madansky (1964); Aczél & Wagner (1980); McConway (1981); Lehrer & Wagner (1983); Genest (1984).

[4] Weisberg and Pettigrew (2023) have recently taken up a similar approach.

in the limited space afforded, but the disconnect between the two traditions we think should no longer be set aside.

Regarding the structure of the Element, Section 2 provides a brief overview of conceptual views on peer disagreement, justified group belief, and group responsibility. In relating the issues to pooling, some questions include: what sort of attitudes should be formed when certain individuals are unreliable indicators of the truth? Rational belief is often said to require justified belief, but how is justifiedness transferred to group belief? Just as individuals can be fit for responsibility, so too can groups. But where does the responsibility lie, and responsibility for what?

In Section 3, we move on to the formal representations of credence and the opinion pooling functions we'll concern ourselves with for the remainder of the Element, along with a set of pooling axioms we might find desirable when seeking a pooling strategy for a particular purpose. The set of axioms is more of an extensive wish list than a coherent set of desiderata. That said, they provide us with precise representations of things that we might intuitively expect pooling mechanisms to possess, which may be reinforced by some brief motivation accompanying each.

In Section 4, we introduce some feasible candidates for pooling opinions. We start things off with the most intuitive strategy, namely *linear pooling*. In short, linear pooling amounts to combining individual opinions through weighted averaging. Situating the pooling rule within the axiomatic tradition, we review the desirable properties from Section 3 that linear pooling functions possess and the axioms they fail to satisfy. We then turn to a class of *multiplicative pooling* strategies, including *geometric pooling*, that tend to be praised for some properties they have that linear pooling lacks. But, as one might imagine, the multiplicative strategies also fall short of having everything we hope for.

After reviewing the linear and multiplicative rules and their properties, we move on to a lesser known approach to pooling opinions, but one that has enjoyed renewed attention in recent years. It generalizes standard credence-based approaches by representing uncertainty not by a single probability function but by a set of probability functions, thus allowing pooled opinions to be *imprecise*. There is a growing literature on imprecise probabilities (IP) in both epistemology and decision theory, including a fascinating volume in this Element series by Paul Weirich (2021). Our focus is on a family of IP pooling models, where pooled opinions are imprecise probabilities, generated from the precise credences of individuals. Under a certain IP model, for instance, if one individual thinks a proposition is 20% likely and another thinks it's 40% likely, their collective opinion might be represented by the closed interval $[0.2, 0.4]$. We likewise proceed to evaluate IP pooling under the axiomatic scheme and showcase some of its unique advantages over linear and multiplicative strategies.

In Section 5, we set aside the impossibilities that arise under the axiomatic approach and think more generally about the end goals of pooling in terms of epistemic rationality. In doing so, we build on previous work from the truth-centered, *accuracy first* program in an effort to identify truth-seeking pooling strategies.[5] We then connect an earlier discussion on justified group belief to some criteria that seemingly promote epistemic rationality via evidentially supported group credences.

After considering epistemic rationality, we turn to practical rationality in Section 6. We attend to a couple of pragmatic arguments supporting certain axioms, which speak against some pooling strategies and in favor of others. Throughout, we relate the practical rationality arguments to an earlier discussion on group responsibility and suggest that the pragmatic arguments point to some collective responsibility when groups decide on how to pool group members' credences.

Section 7 wraps up the Element with a brief summary of recent work focused on relaxing some idealized assumptions. For instance, how can credences be pooled when group members individually consider intersecting, yet different, sets of propositions, and how should groups pool when their individual members aren't probabilistic? We review some methods proposed recently on how to pool credences under such circumstances and finally conclude in Section 8.

Let us reiterate that the present Element is not intended to be a fully comprehensive guide to all the philosophical motivations and pooling strategies one could imagine. But this short Element should provide readers with a sufficient understanding of some philosophical motivations and formal pooling models without presupposing expert-level knowledge in philosophy and mathematics.

2 Philosophical Motivations

Social epistemology has raised various epistemic problems in recent years. We begin with one that seems obviously connected to opinion pooling, namely, *peer disagreement*. Disagreement among a group of individuals serves as the primary motivation for opinion pooling in general, and the unique conditions defining peer disagreement introduce new conceptual challenges concerning the optimal way to handle conflicting credences.

---

[5] See, e.g., Joyce (1998), Pettigrew (2016), and the forthcoming Element by Jason Konek and Ben Levinstein in this series for introductions to the accuracy first program.

After canvassing the problem of epistemic peer disagreement, we turn our attention to *group rationality* and consider some of its aims. Traditional epistemologists tend to hold that rational belief must at least be justified belief. In Section 2.2, we focus on the justification property and how it applies to group belief. We take the general normative claim that rational group belief should be, in part, justified group belief as a motivating reason for endorsing certain pooling axioms and pooling strategies satisfying them. While some pooling axioms can be thought of as aiming at promoting the justifiedness of group credence by satisfactorily incorporating evidence, the conceptual work we review might strengthen their epistemic desirability but also point to some nuances that potentially pose challenges for pooling more generally in obtaining proper epistemic justification.

As a final topic of this section, we consider group responsibility in Section 2.3 and show how it too bears on the evaluation of pooling strategies. Interestingly, this is a relatively unexplored dimension of opinion pooling. This is a bit surprising since group opinions have practical importance in many matters, such as policy decisions, where groups, and possibly individual members, are answerable for the opinions they voice. We review a couple of broad notions of group responsibility that have been defended in the philosophical literature and connect them later to some specific pragmatic issues related to pooling. The upshot is that the pragmatically oriented axioms we'll introduce in Section 3 are more than just mathematical niceties since choosing a pooling strategy can often carry with it certain responsibilities, and these axioms point to a couple of those responsibilities.

2.1 Epistemic Peer Disagreement

In his 2007 paper, "The Epistemology of Disagreement: The Good News," David Christensen presents a case of peer disagreement that has become a staple of the philosophical literature on the topic.

> Suppose that five of us go out to dinner. It's time to pay the check, so the question we're interested in is how much we each owe. We can all see the bill total clearly, we all agree to give a 20 percent tip, and we further agree to split the whole cost evenly, not worrying over who asked for imported water, or skipped dessert, or drank more of the wine. I do the math in my head and become highly confident that our shares are $43 each. Meanwhile, my friend does the math in her head and becomes highly confident that our shares are $45 each. How should I react, upon learning of her belief? (Christensen, 2007, 193)

Before exploring some answers to Christensen's question, some preliminaries are in order. The philosophical debate assumes *symmetry* between individuals, so that all parties involved hold symmetric positions with respect to the body of evidence shared among them. That is, none of the individuals have extra private information the others lack that would be advantageous to their epistemic position. It's further assumed that all individuals hold symmetric positions with respect to their cognitive and epistemic abilities. That is, the individuals involved in a disagreement are assumed to have the same level of cognitive ability and none of the individuals are worse off than any other in terms of truth-seeking capacities, possibly determined by previous track records. Satisfying these assumptions entails that the individuals party to a disagreement are *epistemic peers*.

Epistemic peerhood makes the problem of disagreement especially difficult since all parties would be hard-pressed to deliver a compelling reason why they should dismiss the opinions of the others. Indeed, Christensen argues that you simply cannot dismiss the opinion of another based on the fact that they disagree with you due to what he calls the *independence* condition: ". . . I should assess explanations for the disagreement in a way that's independent of my reasoning on the matter under dispute . . ." (Christensen, 2007, 199). Christensen concludes that upon meeting the independence criterion, and the fact that a peer is just as good at assessing the matter at hand as you are, you (and your peer) are rationally compelled to take the opposing opinion of your peer as evidence against your own opinion. The evidence, in turn, ought to make you less confident in your initial assessment. In the restaurant case, for instance, the opposing conclusions should make you less confident in your answer (and the same goes for your friend), where you should now give equal credence to the hypotheses (193). Revising your epistemic state in such a way amounts to *conciliating*, where you move your opinion toward your peer's (and they move their opinion toward yours). In case of epistemic peerhood, you and your friend are committed to "splitting the difference" (203).

Although *conciliationism*, in general, does not necessarily imply that peers in a disagreement treat all the assessments equally at all times, Adam Elga (2007) has argued that an equal weighting of peer assessments is indeed the only rational response, which he dubbed the *equal weight view*. In his words,

> Suppose that before evaluating a claim, you think that you and your friend are equally likely to evaluate it correctly. When you find out that your friend disagrees with your verdict, how likely should you think it that you are correct? The equal weight view says: 50%. (Elga, 2007, 488)

That is, assuming that the interlocutors are epistemic peers, the equal weight view implies that the probability of each of them being closest to the truth upon learning of their disagreement should be equal. According to Elga, it is absurd to think that a disagreement supplies you with evidence that you are a better judge (486). In the absence of such evidence, you are rationally committed to thinking you and your peer are equally likely to be correct given the nature of epistemic peerhood. So, each must lend equal weight to all the assessments given.

Of course, not everyone agrees with the conciliationist attitude. In his early work on disagreement, Thomas Kelly (2005) defended a *stick to your guns* strategy that is often called the *steadfast view*. We should note that there are many accounts that fall under the steadfast heading, and unfortunately, we can't cover them all, but we'll present two possible candidates here.[6] Among the most radical, the *no independent weight view* says "In at least some cases of peer disagreement, it can be perfectly reasonable to give no weight at all to the opinion of the other party" (Kelly, 2011, 186). While it's unclear whether anyone explicitly endorses the latter view, some views might entail it. Ralph Wedgwood (2007), for example, has argued in favor of privileging the first-person perspective such that one embraces an egocentric bias, or having a fundamental trust in one's own cognitive states (Matheson & Frances, 2018). Strongly embracing an egocentric bias might entail that one completely endorses their own opinion and consequently gives no weight to any peer's opposing opinion.

On an alternative steadfast view, one might retain their initial opinion for the *right reasons*. The *right reasons view* appeals to all the evidence made available to each peer upon learning of a disagreement that includes *first order evidence* (the evidence available prior to learning of the disagreement that pertains to the disputed proposition(s)) and *higher order evidence* (evidence obtained upon learning of a disagreement that pertains to one's reasoning on the matter). The higher order evidence one possesses is that they have a particular belief on the basis of the first order evidence and that their peer has a particular belief on the basis of that same first order evidence. By weighing the higher order evidence equally, peers are not commanded to conciliate or suspend judgement. Rather, weighed equally, the two facts cancel out, leaving each peer with exactly the same evidence before learning of their disagreement. Consequently, the peers retain their initial beliefs, and they do so for the right reasons (see Kelly, 2005).

However, Kelly (2011) has since conceded that the balance between first order and higher order evidence is not always as straightforward as earlier and defends in more recent work the *total evidence view*. The question, though, is how should peers respond to a disagreement if the higher order evidence is not always swamped by the first order evidence? According to Kelly, there is no simple answer to the question. Should the learned higher order evidence speak

---

[6] See, e.g., van Inwagen (1996); Kelly (2005); Huemer (2011); Titelbaum (2015).

strongly in favor of one having made a mistake in their reasoning, they ought to temper their confidence more than if the higher order evidence speaks less strongly in favor of one making a mistake. So, the answer is: it really depends on one's total body of evidence, first order and higher order evidence (Kelly, 2011, 200–202). Proponents of the total evidence view thus reject conciliationism as the universally correct way of responding to a peer disagreement since on some occasions, one should hold *steadfast* in their answer, while on others, they ought to lose a whole lot of confidence. The equal weight view is mistaken then that there's one and only one way that you should revise your opinion in response to a peer disagreement. The total evidence view can thus be seen as a middle ground between steadfastness and conciliationism.

Similarly, Jennifer Lackey's (2010) *justificationist view* might be thought of along the same lines. On her view, what matters most, as the name suggests, is the justification of one's belief. What sets the justificationist view apart from conciliationism is a denial of the independence condition, which Lackey shows to be counterintuitive through the following example.

> Harry and I, who have been colleagues for the past six years, were drinking coffee at Starbucks and trying to determine how many people from our department will be attending the upcoming APA. I, reasoning aloud, say, "Well, Mark and Mary are going on Wednesday, and Sam and Stacey are going on Thursday, and since 2+2=4, there will be four other members of our department at that conference." In response, Harry asserts, 'But 2+2 does not equal 4". (Lackey, 2010, 283)

As Lackey correctly suggests, you should not be rationally required to revise your opinion in the previous case. The overwhelming evidence you have supporting your belief and the personal information you possess about yourself provides evidence that Harry is mistaken. The disagreement, therefore, yields evidence, but not for your mathematical belief. Rather, the disagreement provides evidence for your belief about Harry, which conveys that, in fact, he's not your peer (283). This case also seems to speak in favor of the correctness of the no independent weight view on occasions.

2.1.1 Uniqueness or Permissivism?

We've seen that intuitions apparently clash over which of the responses to peer disagreement is the correct one. This tension is often attributed, in part, to another debate on whether evidence forges a *uniquely* rational response or not. In particular, many have debated the truth of the so-called *uniqueness thesis*.

> Uniqueness Thesis. For any body of evidence, E, and proposition, X, E justifies at most one competitor epistemic attitude toward X.

Richard Feldman (2006) originally proposed and defended the principle in relation to categorical belief – that is, one outright believes a proposition or disbelieves it. Feldman argued that in the context of peer disagreement, the principle entails a skeptical stance, where all parties involved are committed to suspending judgment. But many have argued that categorical belief is too limited to express the epistemic attitudes individuals might hold on some matter, and that skepticism is not always warranted. We can see that with the conciliationist views, given the talk of confidence and (subjective) probability in characterizing beliefs that are taken as graded epistemic attitudes rather than categorical. That's why there's often talk of 'credences' in the epistemology literature, a term that we'll tend to use throughout.

That said, the Uniqueness Thesis, on a more broadly construed interpretation of belief, seems to suggest that there is a uniquely rational graded belief, degree of confidence, subjective probability, or credence that epistemic peers should adopt. The equal weight view, for example, appears to be committed to the thesis since giving equal weight or splitting the difference yields a unique response for all peers. The uniqueness of the attitudes implied by the equal weight view can be further supported by Sinan Dogramaci and Sophie Horowitz's (2016) defense of the Uniqueness Thesis on the grounds that it aids in promoting rationality. In their words,

> Given uniqueness, promoting rationality involves promoting conformity. Conformity allows us to function as epistemic surrogates, which in turn efficiently ensures the reliability of testimony and enables the division of epistemic labor. Our view thus explains why promoting rationality is an effective and efficient means of meeting our epistemic goal, getting to the truth. (Dogramaci & Horowitz, 2016, 139)

It seems that, on their view, the Uniqueness Thesis plays an essential role in promoting rationality by promoting conformity, which ultimately aids individuals in getting closer to the truth. For this reason, we should be inclined to accept the Uniqueness Thesis and consequently the equal weight view.

While promoting rationality might serve as a plausible defense of the Uniqueness Thesis, *permissivists* remain unimpressed. Those who adopt a permissivist stance toward peer disagreement tend to endorse something like the following.

> There is at least one body of total evidence E and proposition P such that multiple credences in P are maximally rational. More precisely, there exist proposition P and probability functions Pr and Pr' such that $Pr(P \mid E)$ $\neq Pr'(P \mid E)$ but both $Pr(P \mid E)$ and $Pr'(P \mid E)$ are maximally rational credences to have in P on body of total evidence E. (Levinstein, 2017, 343)

The total evidence and justificationist views seem to conform to permissivism since peers, on certain occasions, are not committed to adopting a unique attitude in light of a disagreement.[7] Instead, two epistemic peers with differing epistemic attitudes can both be rational. The idea that individuals need not share the same opinions, despite having the same evidence, is, of course, not a novel one. In fact, L. J. Savage (1954) made that very remark many decades ago, ". . . two reasonable individuals faced with the same evidence may have different degrees of confidence in the truth of the same proposition" (3). Savage took this permissivist commitment to be a hallmark of the *personalist* or subjective view of probability.

2.1.2 Peer Disagreement or Not?

Just the same as the competing responses to peer disagreement, we find that intuitions also tend to differ over the (im)permissive nature of responses to the same body of evidence, which may be the cause of diverging intuitions toward responses to peer disagreements. In addition to a clash between intuitions about permissivism and impermissivism, intuitions might also diverge on the basis of one's conception of "peer." In other words, the conflict among social epistemologists might be a mere difference of opinion of whether any given case constitutes a peer disagreement to begin with. We established earlier that peerhood among individuals relies on symmetry with respect to the relevant body of evidence and cognitive and epistemic abilities. But such an account sounds more like a fantasy than reality. Peer disagreements might be hard to come by then in these terms (King, 2012). The epistemic significance of disagreement between two or more seemingly intelligent individuals, however, is not so much a fantasy.

Understood more loosely, "peer" disagreement might prompt different intuitions about how to respond because the term "peer" can be construed in different ways, ranging from a more relaxed view to a highly idealized view that we've so far considered. And from the perspective of each individual that is party to a dispute, as well as the attributer, each person's view could differ on whether there is a peer disagreement, especially if some of the opinions expressed come as a major surprise to all other parties. Recall Lackey's example from earlier. You come to the conclusion that Harry is not a peer after all due to the absurd conclusion he draws. So now, the question has shifted from how to respond to peer disagreements to how to reassess the reliability

---

[7] See also Rosen (2001).

of an interlocutor that will ultimately affect how one responds to the opposing opinion. But how should this be done?

Luc Bovens and Stephan Hartmann (2004) suggested that a proper reassessment can plausibly be captured within a Bayesian framework. We'll skip over the technical details due to the complexity of their notation but invite the reader to take a closer look in their book. What might be useful for our purposes is their *randomization parameter*. In describing this feature, they say, ". . . if witnesses are not reliable, then they are like randomizers. It is as if they do not even look at the state of the world to determine whether the hypothesis is true but rather flip a coin or cast a die to determine whether they will provide a report to the effect that the hypothesis is true. . . On the other hand, if the witnesses are reliable, then they say of what is, that it is and of what is not, that it is not . . ." (57). Accordingly, as the randomization parameter increases, the chance that the witness is unreliable becomes greater. That seems to be the case with Harry. Upon learning his report, you conclude that Harry is more likely to be unreliable (a randomizer) on the matter and therefore less likely to be your peer, leading you to judge his assessment in a more discriminating manner. Bovens and Hartmann's Bayesian evaluative approach can thus help explain how one might reason that the peer linkage is broken in a disagreement, thereby furnishing support for the justificationist view and permissivism more generally.

2.1.3 Peer Disagreement as a Motivation for Pooling

Whatever the right response to peer disagreement is, and whether that response is unique or not, can't be settled here. Our aim is merely to bring to light an important debate in social epistemology and illuminate how it bears on opinion pooling. From our brief summary of the epistemic problem, different views about the correct answer to peer disagreement entail different constraints on pooling strategies. The equal weight view, for example, might imply that there's one and only one uniquely warranted pooling model among a family of models.[8] That is the one that gives fixed and equal weight to all the peer credences. The arguments supporting the equal weight view provide reasons for adopting such a unique pooling mechanism when revising credences individually and forming group-level credences.

---

[8] We note that there are different *types* of pooling methods, for example, linear and multiplicative pooling, and each type is comprised of a family of models. Whether proponents of the equal weight view would agree that different pooling methods are acceptable so long as they impose an equal weight constraint is uncertain. Or, whether they would even concede that the equal weight view is the right answer for forming *group credences* hangs in the balance. Unfortunately, we don't have the answers, but we make note of these uncertainties.

On the other hand, arguments for the total evidence view suggest that the unique equal weight response at the group-level is mistaken since the total evidence (accessible to all) might speak more favorably of some credences than others and thus demand more weight for those and less for others. Since the distribution of weight may be uneven and differ from time to time, the equally weighted pool is merely a special case, but not the correct way to handle every peer disagreement. The arguments supporting the total evidence view provide reasons for adopting a more general pooling strategy that does not already have its weights fixed necessarily by assumption. This similarly goes for the justificationist view, as some credences are sometimes better justified than others. The simple math case illuminates the point, where it turns out that Harry is not your epistemic peer and thus does not deserve equal weight.

We remain uncommitted to there being any one correct pooling strategy for every occasion. But, we point out here that the conceptual work on epistemic peer disagreement can be valuable in motivating some pooling strategies while speaking against others and driving pooling in general.

2.2 Group Rationality and Justified Group Belief

Notice that the problem of peer disagreement focuses on what *individuals* should come to believe. While we're interested in how individuals ought to respond to peer disagreements, we're equally interested in how individuals should form credences *as a group*. These are two different projects, but we contend that pooling strategies can help with both. We should note, however, that group credences generated by means of opinion pooling are often regarded as *epistemic compromises*, merely resulting from the group members' opinions, but not necessarily *consensus* opinions.[9] That is, individuals come to agree on some set of opinions for group reasoning and decision-making purposes, but the members are not necessarily committed to holding those same opinions individually (see Wagner, 2010; Moss, 2011).

Although epistemic compromises do not entail complete epistemic unity among a group's members, we take them to sufficiently represent the attitudes of group agents, and this sentiment appears to be shared by others as we'll come to see shortly. But what good are these group attitudes if they don't guarantee complete epistemic solidarity among a group's members? Following

---

[9] Consensus may be more demanding by requiring a deliberation phase that is iterated over a potentially infinite sequence. See, e.g., DeGroot (1974); Lehrer (1976); Wagner (1978); Hegselmann & Krause (2002).

We also note that group belief need not only arise from epistemic compromise or consensus but alternatively, revolution, conversion, voting, bargaining, and so on (Levi, 1985).

Dogramaci and Horowitz (2016), we might say that conformity via compromise promotes (group) rationality, which gets groups closer to meeting their epistemic goal(s). This sentiment similarly resonates through Matthew Kopec's (2019) goal-oriented view.

> Group Rationality. A particular attitude (behavior, social structure, etc.) is maximally epistemically rational for an agent (or entity) if and only if that attitude (etc.) is amongst the most effective means toward pursuing some specified set of epistemic goals. (Kopec, 2019, 536)

We'll follow Kopec on this goal-oriented view of group rationality, but we'll broaden the scope of goals by including practical goals also.

In sticking with the epistemic dimension for now, what sort of epistemic goals might groups have? Dogramaci and Horowitz pointed out the obvious: getting to the truth.[10] But true belief, whether individually or collectively held, is not the only aim of rational believers. Ever since the days of Plato to the early modern philosophers, like Locke and Hume, epistemologists generally have come to accept that true belief must be supplemented in order to be rational. One supplement is justification. Thus, groups should aim to have *justified true beliefs*. Of course, achieving that is easier said than done. It's hard enough for an individual to hit the epistemic target, let alone a group of individuals with different beliefs and possibly different evidence bases. That said, recent work on the justifiedness of group belief has become a focal point in social epistemology.

2.2.1 Inflationary and Deflationary Accounts

Among the lot of views on group-level justification, Jennifer Lackey (2016) has categorized the most feasible accounts of justified group belief as either *inflationary* or *deflationary*. The inflationary accounts hold that "... groups are treated as entities that can float freely from the epistemic status of their members' beliefs ...," whereas deflationary accounts hold that "... group belief is understood as nothing more than the aggregation of the justified beliefs of the group's members" (342). Some inflationists tend to view group belief as a feature arising from some sort of cohesiveness in the group members' attitudes. For Raimo Tuomela (1992), that cohesive element is *acceptance*: in large part, a group belief in X depends on all operative members jointly accepting X, where 'operative members' is understood as members that jointly intentionally act on behalf of the collective.[11] Margaret Gilbert (2013), by contrast, takes the cohesive element to be *joint commitment*: in large part, a group belief in X

---

[10] We have more to say about the truth aim that we'll get to in Section 5.
[11] See also Schmitt (1994) and Hakli (2011) for variations of the joint acceptance view.

depends on all members being jointly committed to believing X as a body. Although Gilbert has tweaked the precise formulation of this view over past decades, cohesion by joint commitment remains the essential feature. Accordingly, joint commitment is a commitment held by all parties involved, unlike personal commitments that are unilateral, and can only be fulfilled or rescinded by jointly acting together (138). Furthermore, the state of matching wills is *common knowledge* for all parties involved (Gilbert, 2006, 9).[12]

What appears to follow from the joint acceptance and joint commitment views is that the group-level epistemic attitudes yielded are over and above the members' individual beliefs, not just some aggregate. That is, the collective attitude is the product of the *we*, not the *I*. The independence of group belief from the individual members' beliefs can be further illuminated through their function(s) that is often defined by a charter. The US Congress, for example, is a chartered group consisting of elected officials. However, the group making up Congress has no life beyond its office (Schmitt, 1994). The nature of chartered groups conveys the separation of group belief from the individual members' beliefs given that the former is a result of some kind of sanction. Without sanction, however, group beliefs cease to exist, but the individual members' beliefs continue to live on.

While inflationism of group belief seems intuitive when concessions are made and there's some harmony that exists among group members, not everyone agrees. Deflationists alternatively adopt a summative stance toward group belief, where it's the sum or aggregate of some or all of the individual members' beliefs (Lackey, 2016, 358). Alvin Goldman (2014), for instance, offers the following example to support a deflationary, aggregative account of justified group belief.

> G is a group whose members consist of 100 guards (M1-M100) at the British Museum. Each of the first 20 guards, M1-M20, justifiedly believes that guard Albert is planning an inside theft of a famous painting (= A). By deduction from A, each of them infers the (existential) proposition that there is a guard who is planning such a theft (= T). The remaining 80 guards do not believe and are not justified in believing A. Each of the second 20 guards, M21-M40, justifiedly believes that Bernard is planning an inside theft (= B), and deductively infers T from B. The other 80 members do not believe B. Each of a third group of 20 members, M41-M60, justifiedly believes that guard Cecil is planning an inside theft (= C) and deductively infers T from C. The 80 others do not believe C. Thus, 60 members of G (justifiedly) believe T by deduction from some premise he/she justifiedly believes. (Goldman, 2014, 16)

---

[12] Common knowledge is a central concept in game theory involving mutual knowledge spanning higher orders *ad infinitum*: I know that you know that I know that. . .

Whether the group of guards in the earlier example is justified in believing T depends on the dimension we consider. According to Goldman, the group G is not *horizontally* justified in believing T, because there are no other group beliefs resulting from a majority of its members from which T can be deductively inferred. However, G is *vertically* justified in believing T based on the proportion of members who justifiedly believe T (a clear majority). This example is meant to prompt an intuition that justified group belief is deflationary given that G is justified in believing T only when group belief is understood solely in terms of the members' beliefs (the vertical dimension), which Goldman endorses.

Lackey (2016), however, challenges Goldman's summativist account by illustrating that such a majoritarian account is vulnerable to paradox and what she calls the *defeater problem*. With respect to paradox, Lackey's point is a rehearsal of the well-known logical closure paradoxes, that is, the lottery and preface paradoxes.[13] It's pretty easy to see. Based on a majoritarian view of justified group belief, the group of guards justifiedly believes each of the following: not-A, not-B, and not-C. If group belief is closed under entailment, then the group justifiedly believes (not-A & not-B & not-C), yet the group also justifiedly believes (A or B or C), resulting in a contradiction. Relatedly, Lewis Kornhauser and Lawrence Sager (1986) introduced the doctrinal paradox, where proposition-wise majority voting leads to inconsistency, which poses a further problem for summativism when inferring conclusions based on a majority rule. And even if a judgment aggregation function yields a set of logically consistent, closed, and complete set of judgments, Christian List and Philip Pettit (2002) have shown that such a function cannot satisfy a set of reasonable criteria. This is to say, at the very least, that deflationary accounts of justified group belied face some structural problems.

But Lackey thinks that in the guards case, the paradox is less damning than in the individualistic cases of lotteries and prefaces. What she finds more troublesome for summativists is the group's justification for believing T being *defeated* since by entailment, the group justifiedly believes that no one is planning the inside theft, which is an undefeated rebutting (psychological) defeater for the group believing T (Lackey, 2016, 367).[14] For evidentialists and reliabilists

---

[13] See Kyburg (1961) for a description of the lottery paradox and (Makinson, 1965) for a description of the preface paradox.

[14] Lackey defines a psychological defeater as follows: "A psychological defeater is a doubt or belief that is had by S, and indicates that S's belief that p is either false (that is, rebutting) or unreliably formed or sustained (that is, undercutting). Defeaters in this sense function by virtue of being had by S, regardless of their truth-value or epistemic status" (2016, 366).

both, it seems that they would likely accept the following: any group belief formation process should not yield group-level attitudes that are defeated by the evidence possessed by the group. But as Lackey has illustrated, deflationary accounts are susceptible to violating this tenet. The defeater problem, if taken seriously, philosophically challenges deflationism in general, which, in turn, challenges practically all (probabilistic) opinion pooling strategies since opinion pooling falls under the deflationary category.

2.2.2 Are Pooled Credences Unjustified?

Does this mean that pooling strategies are incapable of yielding justified group credences? Not necessarily. Lackey's own view finds a middle ground between inflationism and deflationism. She calls it the *group epistemic agent account*:

> (GEAA). A group G justifiedly believes that p if and only if
>
> (1) A significant percentage of the operative members of G (a) justifiedly believe that p, and (b) are such that adding together the bases of their justified beliefs that p yields a belief set that is coherent.
>
> (2) Full disclosure of the evidence relevant to the proposition that p, accompanied by rational deliberation about that evidence among the members of G in accordance with their individual and group epistemic normative requirements, would not result in further evidence that when added to the bases of G's members' beliefs that p, yields a total belief set that fails to make sufficiently probable that p. (Lackey, 2016, 381)

GEAA is an account of justification for categorical group beliefs, but perhaps we can formulate a plausible credal version. GEAA (1a) concerns the justification of the individual attitudes, while (1b) concerns the bases of those attitudes. In the credal case, (1a) just says that a significant percentage of the operative members have justified credences, while (1b) says the conjunction of their evidence is consistent. What about GEAA (2)? Here's a version stated for epistemic attitudes more generally: upon members disclosing their evidence in rational deliberation, the group-level attitudes resulting from the members' attitudes individually conditioned on the shared evidence, E, should not be inconsistent with the group-level attitudes (formed from the member's unconditional attitudes) conditioned on E. If plausible, then GEAA (2) spells good news for justified group credence via pooling. Indeed, we'll introduce a criterion in Section 3 to that effect, namely, *External Bayesianity*, and show in Section 4 which pooling strategies meet the demand.

2.2.3 Justifiedness as an Evaluative Criterion

Just like the problem of peer disagreement, we can't settle the debate on justified group belief in this Element. However, what the reader should take away from the discussion is that justifiedness is a fundamental feature of rational group belief/credence. Some criteria we'll introduce in due course aim at conferring justifiedness to pooled credences in line with GEAA as interpreted. The pooling strategies satisfying such criteria consequently are consistent with promoting Group Rationality in meeting at least one epistemic goal. Of course, the inflationary/deflationary and categorical/credal distinctions and assimilating views leave open philosophical questions on the broader matter of justified group belief. But we hope that casting light on the issue in this Element at least gets the ball rolling.

2.3 Group Rationality and Responsibility

Taken as *agents* in their own right, groups should not only aim to fulfill their epistemic goals, as Group Rationality requires, but their practical goals also. For why else should individuals be willing to compromise or reach a consensus if the group opinions of the group agent are not put to use in practice? If this is right, then Group Rationality should be broadened to cover the practical interests of groups also, which we'll assume from here on.[15]

Furthermore, Group Rationality leaves open 'attitude', which might generally mean intentional attitude. Intentional attitudes, for example, beliefs and desires, then ought to be the most instrumentally effective in meeting a group's epistemic goals. But again, epistemic goals aren't the only things groups care about and thus, intentional attitudes are collectively rational by being most instrumentally effective in also meeting a group's practical goals. If correct, collective attitudes set up for group action as the pillars of means-end practical reasoning.[16] In turn, the actions performed by groups, like the actions performed by individuals, yield consequences that they can be held accountable for. Intentional group attitudes leading to group action make groups fit for responsibility.

---

[15] Whether groups constitute agents in their own right is a controversial issue. Christian List and Philip Pettit (2011) defend the affirmative, suggesting that groups can constitute agents that float freely from their members. We're neutral on the matter, especially since pooling is not motivated only from a group agency standpoint. Recall from the introduction that we said pooling can serve different functions, like summarizing individual opinions. But of course, one function can be in forming credences on behalf of group agents. This section on responsibility focuses on that perspective.

[16] We assume a consequentialist-like picture in the background rather than Kantian or Aristotelian.

2.3.1 Responsibility for What?

But what does it mean for a group to act? Margaret Gilbert's account on joint commitment mentioned earlier provides a nice starting point in answering this question. On Gilbert's (2006) view, to collectively act means the following:

> Group Action. Persons X and Y are collectively doing A if and only if they collectively intend to do A,[17] and each is effectively acting, in light of the associated joint commitment, so as to bring about fulfillment of this intention. (Gilbert, 2006, 12)

Joint commitment centrally establishes a unifying bond between group members with respect to collective action, as a joint commitment provides all members with reason as a body to perform some act. The bond by joint commitment consequently makes members answerable to one another in case of defaulting on the commitment, and owing conformity to all other parties (11). These consequences of joint commitment seemingly engender some form of responsibility on behalf of a group's members, particularly in fulfilling their joint commitment.

The general idea of there being some cohesive commitment spanning the individual members of groups seems to be a necessary element in determining a group's fitness for responsibility. Raimo Tuomela and Pekka Mäkelä (2016) have similarly argued along this line, suggesting that groups can be characterized by an *ethos* that unites the members through a commitment to conforming to it. No member can act against the group's ethos, and the ethos can only be abolished through collective decision-making (301). So, like Gilbert's view, rescinding the commitment can't be done by any one individual but rather jointly by the collective.

As a group's ethos is often broadly encompassing, a multitude of virtues can be held under it. For our purposes, we might suggest that a commitment to promoting Group Rationality (extended to practical goals) is one such virtue of an ideal group ethos. The commitment makes group members responsible for honoring it and accountable for defaulting on their responsibility. Groups are then collectively responsible for the intentional attitudes they hold and actions they perform. We should note, however, that the responsibility considered here is not necessarily moral responsibility. Rather, it's a bit broader as a commitment to conforming to norms that need not be moral per se. Most central in this context are rationality norms that promote the interests of a group and its members. A failure to promote such interests individually and as a group is

---

[17] Collective intention is meant here as a joint commitment to intend as a body to perform some action. And the matching state of wills is common knowledge among all parties.

what members and the group are answerable for. Having said that, let's specify further where the responsibility lies.

2.3.2 Responsibility for Who?

Tuomela and Mäkelä suggest that the responsibility trickles down to the individual members:

> As the group's actions are constituted by its members' actions, the group will be responsible also for its members' participatory actions (and lack of them in other cases). This kind of group responsibility involves that the members of a we-mode group are responsible for their own participatory actions as well as typically to an extent responsible also for the other members' participatory actions ... (Tuomela & Mäkelä, 2016, 309)

Group responsibility on their view is reductive. That is, group responsibility reduces to the individual responsibility of each member, and individual responsibility is twofold, applying to each member's own behavior as well as the participatory behavior of others. This view might be stronger than Gilbert's, as a group's members are not just answerable for their own behavior but to an extent, the behavior of other members also, giving rise to some sort of a "guilty by association" attribution. While admittedly stringent, the view is sensible in some instances such as when a group of criminals commits an illegal act. The group as a whole may be held accountable in case all members were willing participants and aware of the others' involvement because they could have intervened to obstruct the activity.

What might further compel one to adopt a reductive stance is the *complicity* of group members, as they are bounded by the commitment to the ethos. Thus, members cannot escape or separate themselves from the group's intentional attitudes and resulting group actions because of the general commitment to the ethos, which is unbreakable by any one dissenter. Group members are therefore complicit not only in the actions taken but also in the formation of the group's intentional attitudes, as they are all jointly committed to the ethos, for example, promoting Group Rationality, and consequently jointly committed to the intentional attitudes adopted. Actual organizations seem to provide evidence for this claim: ACLU, Catholic Church, Sierra Club, and so on.

But what does it mean to be complicit? As Christopher Kutz (2000) has suggested, intentional participation, independent of any actual difference one makes, is enough for one to be complicit. Kutz's view seems to support the earlier claim that group members are complicit when committed to the ethos and jointly committed to adopting certain intentional attitudes. This is because fulfilling a commitment to the ethos and any following joint commitments involves intentional participation. And since the difference any one member makes is independent, the active intention to make good on the joint duties suffices to make one complicit. Notice that Kutz's view takes a more agent-relational approach to defining complicity, separating it from mere causal responsibility that is limited in scope.[18]

2.3.3 Responsible Pooling

How does the discussion here bear on opinion pooling? From a group agency perspective, if all group members jointly accept or are committed to some group attitude formation procedure, then all members bear some level of responsibility for the group opinions formed and any acts performed under those opinions. Should bad outcomes obtain that are consequential of the type of group attitudes formed, the members are complicit according to the given view, as they are intentional participants. If correct, groups need to take care in selecting a pooling strategy, especially if Group Rationality is taken as part of a group's ethos.

In the next section, we'll introduce a handful of pooling axioms that are epistemically and practically motivated, which stand in support of promoting Group Rationality. However, we'll come to learn in Section 4 that satisfying all of the axioms is no easy task. There are also tensions between promoting epistemic goals and promoting practical goals. These issues will become more apparent in Sections 5 and 6. For now, we only want to suggest that group responsibility cannot be ignored in evaluating pooling strategies, as the choice of pooling strategy in a given situation determines certain intentional attitudes of the group that they are answerable for holding and acting under.

What we find interesting is that there is little to no discussion of group responsibility in the literature. On our view, this is surprising since group opinions have enormous social influence; for example, the opinions of a political party, and so pooling strategies should not be evaluated independent of a normative domain to which they belong.[19] Thus, group responsibility is a nontrivial issue for opinion pooling and should be welcomed in the evaluation of pooling strategies. Again, we're very limited in what we can say here, but we hope to prompt future work on the relation.

---

[18] See Bazargan-Forward (2017) for a more recent agent-relational account that separates complicity from causal accounts. List and Pettit (2011) similarly reject causal responsibility, which allows for complex entities such as corporations, treated as group agents, to be fit for responsibility.

[19] More recently, a strong case has been made for an intimate relationship between the epistemic status and relevant moral implications of holding particular beliefs known as *moral encroachment* (see, e.g., Moss, 2018; Basu, 2019; Jorgensen Bolinger, 2020).

3 Desirable Features of Pooling Strategies

In Section 2, we raised some philosophical problems that are informative when we come to evaluate pooling strategies, particularly when we ask which promote epistemic and practical aims. We'll revisit those points from time to time. But let's now get acquainted with the formal representations of credences and pooling strategies we'll assume throughout, followed by the properties we often want our pooling strategies to have.

3.1 The Formal Framework

Let's begin with the individuals. To represent an individual's opinions on a certain matter, we must represent the propositions about which they have an opinion as well as their opinions about them. Conforming to the standard parlance of philosophical decision theory and epistemology, we represent a proposition as a set of possible worlds. Until Section 7, we assume there is a finite set of possible worlds, $\mathscr{W} = \{w_1, \ldots, w_n\}$, grained as finely as needed to represent the individual's opinions, but no finer, and that the individual assigns credences to each element of the full algebra $\mathscr{A}$ of subsets of $\mathscr{W}$. Given X and Y in $\mathscr{A}$, we write $X \vee Y$ for the union of X and Y, $X \wedge Y$ for their intersection, and $\neg X$ for the complement of X.

Next, we represent the individuals' opinions about these propositions by a function $P : \mathscr{A} \rightarrow [0, 1]$, which takes each proposition X in $\mathscr{A}$ and returns $P(X)$, the individual's unconditional credence in X. Until Section 7, we assume P satisfies the Kolmogorov axioms for probabilities: that is, $P(\mathscr{W}) = 1$, $P(\emptyset) = 0$, and $P(X \vee Y) = P(X) + P(Y)$ whenever X and Y are disjoint.

We also write $P(X | Y)$ for the individual's conditional credence in X given Y, and define it using the so-called Ratio Formula: if $P(Y) > 0$,

$$P(X | Y) = \frac{P(X \wedge Y)}{P(Y)}$$

Otherwise, it is undefined.

At various points, we will refer to Bayes' Rule, which is the standard method for updating a probability function upon receipt of some new evidence that comes in the form of a proposition learned with certainty. It says that your new unconditional credence in a proposition should be your old conditional credence in it given the evidence you've learned. That is, for an individual with probability function P, upon learning E, their new credence in X should be $P(X | E)$.

Turning our attention now to groups. Suppose we have a group of individuals $i = 1, \ldots, n$. Until Section 7, we assume each individual i has opinions that are represented by a probability function P_i on the same agenda $\mathscr{A}$. We write $\Delta_{\mathscr{A}}$

for the set of all probability functions on $\mathscr{A}$, and $\Delta^n_{\mathscr{A}}$ for the set of sequences $(P_1, \ldots, P_n)$ of n probability functions on $\mathscr{A}$. We call such a sequence an *opinion profile*. A *pooling strategy* is a function $F : \Delta^n_{\mathscr{A}} \to \Delta_{\mathscr{A}}$. In other words, F is a function that takes an opinion profile, which is a sequence of probability functions, one for each member of the group, to a single probability function, which represents the collective credences of the group. (When there is no ambiguity, we drop the subscript and write Δ and Δ^n instead of $\Delta_{\mathscr{A}}$ and $\Delta^n_{\mathscr{A}}$.)

In Section 4.4, we consider a more general representation of collective credences that uses *imprecise probabilities*.

With the basic framework now in place, we present a wish list of desirable criteria we would like a pooling strategy F to meet before taking the plunge into the abyss of infinitely many pooling strategies. So, let us begin with some staples from the philosophical and statistical literatures that have been given as part of the so-called axiomatic approach.

3.2 Preserving Unanimous Judgments

The first concerns agreement. There are two versions; the first is strictly stronger than the second.

> **(Local) Unanimity Preservation.** For all probability functions $P_1, \ldots, P_n$ on $\mathscr{A}$, and for all propositions X in $\mathscr{A}$, if $P_1(X) = \cdots = P_n(X)$, then
>
> $$F(P_1, \ldots, P_n)(X) = P_1(X) = \cdots = P_n(X)$$

That is, if all individuals agree about *some* proposition, the pool should agree with them about that proposition.

> **(Global) Unanimity Preservation.** For all probability functions $P_1, \ldots, P_n$ on $\mathscr{A}$, if, for all propositions $X \in \mathscr{A}$, $P_1(X) = \cdots = P_n(X)$, then for all X in $\mathscr{A}$,
>
> $$F(P_1, \ldots, P_n)(X) = P_1(X) = \cdots = P_n(X)$$

That is, if all individuals agree about *all* propositions, the pool should agree with them about those propositions.

If group members find themselves agreeing with one another, the unanimity criteria demand that the agreement is maintained after pooling. As we know, agreement is often hard to come by; these criteria say that groups should take advantage of it when they can. That being said, relaxing the constraints may be necessary if individuals have different private evidence (Dietrich & List, 2015), since each might have evidence that supports a particular proposition strongly, but which, when combined, refutes it.

3.3 Eventwise Independence

The second criterion concerns the independence of a group's credence in a proposition from the individual credences of all other propositions in the agenda:

> **Eventwise Independence.**[20] There exists a function $G : \mathscr{A} \times [0,1]^n \to [0,1]$ such that for all probability functions $P_1, \ldots, P_n$ on $\mathscr{A}$, and for all propositions X in $\mathscr{A}$,
>
> $$F(P_1, \ldots, P_n)(X) = G(X, P_1(X), \ldots, P_n(X))$$

This criterion is also known as the *weak setwise function property*, which is equivalent to the *marginalization property* (McConway, 1981), and *neutrality* (Dietrich & List, 2017). The idea is that the group credence for any proposition X should depend only on the group members' credences in X; it should not depend on their individual credences about anything else. It would be unusual, epistemically, if this weren't the case. Say, for example, that the collective evaluates the propositions that a coin flip results in heads face up and that the global average surface temperature reaches a new record high in 2023. Whatever way the collective chooses to pool, the group credence for the coin landing heads should not depend on the members' credences concerning the global average surface temperature.[21]

3.4 Ruling Out Dictators

The third criterion is based on a principle of welfare economics (Arrow, 1951), but for our purposes, we're interested in the epistemic implications:

> **Non-Dictatorship.** There is no individual i such that for all probability functions $P_1, \ldots, P_n$ on $\mathscr{A}$, $F(P_1, \ldots, P_n) = P_i$.

Why care about Non-Dictatorship? Of course, it depends on why you are using the pooling function. If your purpose is to give a summary of the opinions among the individuals in the group, Non-Dictatorship lays down the plausible principle that no good summary depends only on a single individual's view. Similarly, if you wish to use the pooled opinions to make a decision on behalf of the group that all members can get behind and for which they are happy to be held responsible, and if the members of the group share the same evidence, but have different posterior credences because they don't share the same prior, then

---

[20] Dietrich and List (2015) call G the *local pooling criteria*.

[21] We'll revisit independence again shortly when we meet an additional criterion.

again Non-Dictatorship lays down a plausible principle. But there are also cases where we can legitimately violate it. Perhaps you will use the pooled opinion to choose on behalf of the group, and the group members all have the same prior, but one member has all the evidence that the others have and maybe even some more on top of that: perhaps they're the head of an intelligence organization who sees all the intelligence reports, while all the other members of the group are intelligence officers who each see only some. Then in that case there seems no problem with electing them the dictator.

3.5 Bounding the Group's Opinions

In the same vein, the fourth criterion might be seen as a constraint motivated by the same epistemic goal but more explicit in its direction:

Boundedness.[22] For all probability functions $P_1, \ldots, P_n$ on $\mathscr{A}$, and for all propositions X in $\mathscr{A}$,

$$\min(P_1(X), \ldots, P_n(X)) \leq F(P_1, \ldots, P_n)(X) \leq \max(P_1(X), \ldots, P_n(X))$$

By treating group members' credences as evidence, the group's total evidence signals that the evidentially supported group credence lies somewhere in the range of individual credences. Boundedness ensures that pooling does not yield group credences outside of the range and thus respects the group's total evidence. Besides respecting the evidence, empirical work on collective intelligence has demonstrated that groups often *bracket the truth* (Soll & Larrick, 2009). Thus, pooling strategies abiding by Boundedness promote Group Rationality in two ways: respecting the evidence and getting closer to the truth (more on the latter in Section 5). Furthermore, since Boundedness implies Unanimity Preservation, pooling rules satisfying the former consequently satisfy the latter.

While Boundedness appears to be an intuitive constraint, Easwaran et al. (2016) have appealed to an intuitive case by Christensen (2009) to argue it isn't always desirable. Suppose that a doctor is 97% confident about the right dosage of a drug to administer to a patient. The doctor learns that their equally qualified colleague is 96% confident about the same dosage for that patient. Christensen concludes that in this case, learning that a colleague is also very confident about the dosage should boost, not lower, the doctor's confidence in the dosage being correct. If we take this intuition to hold in the context of pooling the two doctors' opinions, the pooled opinion would indeed lie outside the range and to the right of the interval on the real line. And such violations of

---

[22] The constraint is also called *the reasonable range* (Elkin & Wheeler, 2018).

Boundedness are even more compelling when the individuals have different private information (Dietrich, 2010).

3.6 The Interaction of Pooling and Learning

The next criterion concerns pooling and learning. We described earlier an application of Bayesian learning in assessing the reliability of others. Given its prominence in many scientific fields, and its dominance as a rule for learning in formal epistemology and decision and game theory, Bayes' rule for updating on new information can be regarded as a fundamental norm for both individual and collective rationality in general – recall: it says that, upon learning a proposition E, your new unconditional credence in X should be your old conditional credence in X given E. What's more, there are many arguments to the effect that it is the sole rational way for an individual or a group to update their credal opinions: updating in this way maximizes expected accuracy (Greaves & Wallace, 2006); it is the only way to avoid being accuracy dominated (Briggs & Pettigrew, 2020; Nielsen, 2021); it is the only way to avoid being vulnerable to a diachronic Dutch Book (Lewis, 1999). In light of this, any pooling strategy adopted by a group should play nicely with Bayesian learning, especially if Group Rationality is taken to be part of the group's ethos. One consequence of the interplay is that it should make no difference whether all individuals update on the same evidence and pool their updated credences, or whether they pool their individual credences and then update the pool on the evidence.

> **External Bayesianity.** For all probability functions $P_1, \ldots, P_n$ on $\mathscr{A}$ and for all propositions X and E in $\mathscr{A}$,
>
> $$F(P_1(-\,|\,E), \ldots, P_n(-\,|\,E))(X) = F(P_1, \ldots, P_n)(X\,|\,E)$$
>
> where $P_i(-\,|\,E)$ is the probability function obtained from P_i by updating on E using Bayes' Rule.
>
> That is, the following diagram should commute:

$$
\begin{array}{ccc}
(P_1,\ldots,P_n) & \xrightarrow{\;\text{update on } E\;} & (P_1(-\,|\,E),\ldots,P_n(-\,|\,E)) \\
{\scriptstyle\text{pool using } F}\Big\downarrow & & \Big\downarrow{\scriptstyle\text{pool using } F} \\
F(P_1,\ldots,P_n)\!\!\!\xrightarrow[\text{update on } E]{} & \begin{array}{l} F(P_1(-\,|\,E),\ldots,P_n(-\,|\,E))(-) \\ = F(P_1,\ldots,P_n)(-\,|\,E) \end{array}
\end{array}
$$

To drive the intuition, suppose you wish to determine whether a group is responsible for some harm caused by a decision that they made collectively – perhaps they're the board of a corporation whose products caused injury and they're liable if their corporate credence that this would happen is above some threshold. To do this, you need to determine what the group's credences were in a range of relevant propositions, and you hope to ascribe those group credences, which attached to the collective agent that is the group, rather than to any of the individuals, by using a pooling strategy. Then it seems you'll want that pooling function to satisfy External Bayesianity. If it doesn't, it's possible that it will ascribe different credences to the group depending on whether you update the individuals on the group's evidence and then pool the posteriors or pool the priors and update them on the group's evidence. And that sort of arbitrariness might well undermine your claim that the group is liable based on the credence you ascribe – perhaps they are if you use the group credences derived from pooling then update, but not if you update first then pool. And even if both give credences that render them liable, it's plausible that the group is *more* liable, and therefore deserving of a *more* severe rebuke, the *higher* their credence. So the credence itself matters, not just whether it lies above some threshold.

3.7 Preserving Judgments of Independence

Our sixth criterion maintains that, after pooling, there should be no probabilistic correlation established between propositions that all members of the group judge beforehand to be probabilistically independent:

Probabilistic Independence Preservation. For all probability functions $P_1, \ldots, P_n$ on $\mathscr{A}$, if, for all $i = 1, \ldots, n$ and X, Y in $\mathscr{A}$ such that $P(Y) > 0$, $P_i(X \mid Y) = P_i(X)$, then

$$F(P_1, \ldots, P_n)(X \mid Y) = F(P_1, \ldots, P_n)(X)$$

Probabilistic Independence Preservation, like Bayesian learning, shields groups from being Dutch Booked in some form. As Henry Kyburg and Michael Pittarelli (1996) illustrated, if Probabilistic Independence Preservation is violated, then there exists a book of bets that the group will find acceptable but that guarantees they'll lose money come what may.[23] Whatever values each individual holds, it's reasonable to assume that all group members prefer not to exchange bets on propositions in the agenda that result in such a loss. Indeed, any group that takes Group Rationality as part of its ethos should be committed to Probabilistic Independence Preservation, for its violation by a chosen pooling strategy strictly goes against it.

---

[23] See also Elkin and Wheeler (2018) for a variation of the argument in the context of peer disagreement. We give a detailed version of the argument in Section 6.

3.8 No Regrets

Similar in spirit, our final criterion concerns an expected and unnecessary loss from "throwing away money," so to speak, by overpaying for bets or underselling them. Call the loss *ex ante regret*. Let each probability function P_i for $i = 1, \ldots, n$ induce a pair of regret functions, $r_{P_i}^-(\cdot, \cdot)$ and $r_{P_i}^+(\cdot, \cdot)$, that represent the *ex ante* regret of trading bets under P_i that pay one monetary unit if $X \in \mathscr{A}$ is true and zero otherwise. Each function maps a price-proposition pair $(u, X) \in [0, \infty) \times \mathscr{A}$, relative to P_i, to a real number, and we assume throughout that they take the functional forms $r_{P_i}^-(u, X) = \max\{u - P_i(X), 0\}$ and $r_{P_i}^+(v, X) = \max\{P_i(X) - v, 0\}$.

For $u \in [0, \infty)$ and $X \in \mathscr{A}$, $r_{P_i}^-(u, X)$ is the *ex ante* regret of buying a bet on X for a price u and $r_{P_i}^+(u, X)$ is the *ex ante* regret of selling a bet on X for a price u, relative to P_i. Considering the *ex ante* regrets with respect to trading bets for all individuals $i = 1, \ldots, n$, pooling strategies should ensure the following:

> **No Regrets.** For all probability functions $P_1, \ldots, P_n$ on $\mathscr{A}$, for all propositions X in $\mathscr{A}$, and for all individuals $i = 1, \ldots, n$,
>
> - $r_{P_i}^-(F(P_1, \ldots, P_n)^-(X), X) = 0$, and
> - $r_{P_i}^+(F(P_1, \ldots, P_n)^+(X), X) = 0$.

That's to say all individuals i should have no *ex ante* regrets of trading bets at the group's maximum buying price $F(P_1, \ldots, P_n)^-(X) = \min F(P_1, \ldots, P_n)(X)$ and minimum selling price $F(P_1, \ldots, P_n)^+(X) = \max F(P_1, \ldots, P_n)(X)$ for all $X \in \mathscr{A}$. Given that the most common pooling strategies return a single probability function, $F(P_1, \ldots, P_n)^-(X) = F(P_1, \ldots, P_n)^+(X) = F(P_1, \ldots, P_n)(X)$.[24] We'll extend pooling strategies later on, where the pooling mechanism returns a set of probability functions that need not be a singleton set, that is, the credences may be *imprecise*.

From a practical standpoint, the No Regrets criterion should be quite intuitive, as no rational individual, in general, should be willing to pay a price above an asset's perceived value when buying it, nor should the individual be willing to accept a price below the perceived value of the asset when selling it. In other words, individuals should neither happily expect to *overpay* for an asset nor *undersell* it. That just seems to be a bit of common sense. Although the constraint is quite strong, as it quantifies over all individuals, it is plausible when the individuals are epistemic peers (Elkin & Wheeler, 2018) or if the group is held liable for decisions made under the group's credences since the group must

---

[24] In other words, the most common pooling strategies yield *fair* prices such that the bettor is indifferent to taking a bet for/against $X \in \mathscr{A}$ and abstaining (Vicig & Seidenfeld, 2012, 9).

answer for any bad deals made upon violating it when at least one individual signaled so much all along.

In the next section, we'll attend to the pooling axioms provided here and learn, unsurprisingly, that not all of them play nicely with one another. But evaluating pooling strategies beyond mere impossibility results will be a goal of ours in the coming pages, illuminating the context-dependency of some criteria. This will be, in part, motivated by the earlier philosophical discussions. With any luck, our unifying approach might inspire others to look beyond mere technical difficulties and consider the instrumental value of pooling strategies based on the epistemic and practical interests and needs of groups in different circumstances.

4 Opinion Pooling Strategies

Now that we've laid out a handful of properties that we'd like our pooling strategies to have, let's meet some of the strategies themselves. We'll first consider two families: the linear pooling strategies, and the multiplicative pooling strategies (of which the geometric pooling strategies are a subfamily). The linear pooling strategies are perhaps the ones that occur to us first when we try to formulate a way to aggregate credences, and they boast a number of desirable features, many of which are unique to them. But there are features they lack, and we look to the multiplicative rules to find ones that have those features. After wrapping up our discussion of linear and multiplicative pooling, the approaches that focus on precise probabilities, we turn to methods that appeal to imprecise probabilities. While the latter boast an even greater number of features than the classical strategies, we'll come to find that in the end, only one gets us everything.

4.1 Linear Pooling

Earlier, we met epidemiologists Anya, Bon, and Carys who are, respectively, 20%, 60%, and 70% sure that polio will be completely eradicated by 2030. How sure are they as a group? If they were to act as a group, perhaps by deciding how much funding a government should plan to spend on care for polio patients in the future, which credences should they use? If they were to be held responsible as a group, perhaps for that funding planning decision, which credences should we attribute to them? If we're to summarize their views as a single credence to give some third party some information about views within the group, which should we use?

A natural answer to all of these questions is to say that we should take the average of their credences; or, more precisely, their *arithmetic mean*. That is, we should say that, as a group, Anya, Bon, and Carys have credence $\frac{1}{3}0.2 + \frac{1}{3}0.6 + \frac{1}{3}0.7 = 0.5$ that polio will be eradicated by 2030.

Here is the pooling strategy in greater generality:

Straight Linear Pooling Suppose $P_1, \ldots, P_n$ are probabilistic credence functions defined on the same agenda $\mathscr{A}$. Then, for any X in $\mathscr{A}$,

$$\mathrm{LP}(P_1, \ldots, P_n)(X) = \frac{1}{n}P_1(X) + \cdots + \frac{1}{n}P_n(X)$$

That is, the straight linear pool's credence in X is simply the average of the individuals' credence in X. Notice that Straight Linear Pooling serves as a natural candidate for pooling under the equal weight view and may be epistemically motivated by such an account (Jehle & Fitelson, 2009).

But straight linear pooling is just one member of a larger family of strategies. In straight linear pooling, the same weight is afforded to each individual's opinion. In the larger family, these weights can vary, which might be motivated by permissivist views like the justificationist and total evidence views. For instance, in the case of epidemiologists earlier, we might decide to give less weight to Carys, because her work is not directly on polio itself, while Anya's and Bon's is. So perhaps Anya receives weight $2/5$, rather than $1/3$, and Bon receives the same, but Carys receives $1/5$, rather than $1/3$. Then the weighted linear pool of their credences is $\frac{2}{5}0.2 + \frac{2}{5}0.6 + \frac{1}{5}0.7 = 0.46$.

So, to specify a specific pooling strategy in this family, we have to specify the weight that each individual will receive. A weight is a nonnegative real number, and the weights for all the individuals must add up to 1. So, if $P_1, \ldots, P_n$ are the probabilistic credence functions of the individuals in the group, then a sequence of weights is a sequence $\Lambda = (\lambda_1, \ldots, \lambda_n)$, where $0 \leq \lambda_1, \ldots, \lambda_n \leq 1$ and $\lambda_1 + \cdots + \lambda_n = 1$. In the previous paragraph, the sequence of weights for Anya, Bon, and Carys was $(2/5, 2/5, 1/5)$. So here is the generalization of linear pooling, tracing back at least to Stone (1961):

Linear Pooling Suppose $P_1, \ldots, P_n$ are probabilistic credence functions defined on the same agenda $\mathscr{A}$; and suppose $\Lambda = (\lambda_1, \ldots, \lambda_n)$ is a sequence of weights. Then, for any X in $\mathscr{A}$,

$$\mathrm{LP}^{\Lambda}(P_1, \ldots, P_n)(X) = \lambda_1 P_1(X) + \cdots + \lambda_n P_n(X)$$

Note: If $P_1, \ldots, P_n$ are probabilistic credence functions, then $\mathrm{LP}^{\Lambda}(P_1, \ldots, P_n)$ is a probabilistic credence function as well.

We say that LP^{Λ} is *dictatorial* if one individual gets all the weight, that is, if $\lambda_i = 1$ for some i and $\lambda_j = 0$ for all $j \neq i$. In that case, for any X in $\mathscr{A}$,

$$\mathrm{LP}^{\Lambda}(P_1, \ldots, P_n)(X) = P_i(X)$$

Individual *i* is then a dictator for that group – what they say goes! Assuming Non-Dictatorship, such a pooling strategy must be ruled out, but on the other hand, the case of Harry from Section 2.1 provides a compelling instance where we might relax the constraint and accept the latter strategy. But let's set that issue aside for now.

To evaluate the linear pooling strategies, let's focus our attention on the axioms from Section 3 that these pooling strategies satisfy, which they don't, and whether there are any combinations of these axioms that these pooling strategies alone satisfy.

Each linear pooling strategy LP^Λ satisfies the following axioms:

(1a) *Local Unanimity Preservation*

Why? The arithmetic mean of n copies of the same number is just that number.

(1b) *Global Unanimity Preservation*

Why? This follows from Local Unanimity Preservation.

(2) *Eventwise Independence*

Why? The pooled credence in a proposition is always just the weighted average of the individual credences in that proposition. In order to calculate the linear pool's credence in a proposition, you don't need to know the individuals' credences in anything other than that proposition.

(3) *Boundedness*

Why? The weighted average of a sequence of numbers is always at least as great as the smallest in the sequence and at most as great as the largest.

Rather unsurprisingly, the only weighted linear pooling strategies that satisfy the following are non-dictatorial ones:

(4) *Non-Dictatorship*

Why? The clue is in the name!

The only weighted linear pooling strategies that satisfy External Bayesianity and Probabilistic Independence Preservation are dictatorial:

(5) *External Bayesianity*

Why? This follows from a theorem by Madansky (1964), which says that the only way to ensure that a linear pooling strategy will commute with Bayesian updating on evidence regardless of the individual credence functions it is fed is to make it dictatorial, so that there is one individual whose opinions always give the group's opinions, no matter what they are, or what the other individuals think. To see that linear pooling violates External Bayesianity, it's sufficient to give Madansky's theorem for the case of two individuals.[25]

Theorem 1 (Madansky, 1964). *Suppose that*

(a) *P, Q are probabilistic credence functions defined on $\mathscr{A}$,*
(b) *$\Lambda = (\lambda, 1 - \lambda)$ is a sequence of weights,*
(c) *X and E are propositions in $\mathscr{A}$,*
(d) *$P(E), Q(E) > 0$,*

Then, if

$$LP^{\Lambda}(P, Q)(X|E) = LP^{\Lambda}(P(- \mid E), Q(- \mid E))(X)$$

Then at least one of the following must be true:

(i) *Λ is dictatorial. That is, $\lambda = 0$ or $\lambda = 1$.*
(ii) *$P(X|E) = Q(X|E)$. That is, all individuals agree on how likely X is given E.*
(iii) *$P(E) = Q(E)$. That is, all individuals agree on how likely E is.*

Given that it is easy to specify P, Q, along with X and E, such that (ii) and (iii) don't hold, it follows that, if linear pooling with weights Λ commutes with conditionalization, then (i) must be true and Λ is dictatorial.

(6) *Probabilistic Independence Preservation*
Why? This follows from a theorem that is in the background in Laddaga (1977) and Lehrer & Wagner (1983). It says that it is extremely rare for linear pooling to preserve judgments of independence, and only dictatorial versions guarantee it. A probabilistic credence function P takes two propositions X and Y to be independent iff $P(X \wedge Y) = P(X)P(Y)$.[26]

Theorem 2 (Laddaga, 1977; Lehrer & Wagner, 1983). *Suppose that*

(a) *P, Q are probabilistic credence functions defined on $\mathscr{A}$,*
(b) *$\Lambda = (\lambda, 1 - \lambda)$ is a sequence of weights,*
(c) *X and Y are propositions in $\mathscr{A}$.*

Then, if

(1) *P and Q both take X and Y to be independent, and*
(2) *$LP^{\Lambda}(P, Q)$ takes X and Y to be independent.*

---

[25] We sketch the proof of this result in the Appendix.
[26] We sketch the proof in the Appendix.

Then at least one of the following must be true:

  (i) Λ *is dictatorial. That is,* $\lambda = 0$ *or* $\lambda = 1;$
  (ii) $P(X) = Q(X)$. *That is, the individuals agree on how likely X is.*
  (iii) $P(Y) = Q(Y)$. *That is, the individuals agree on how likely Y is.*

Lastly, no linear pooling function satisfies

(7) *No Regrets*

  Why? Suppose that $P_i \neq P_j$ for some individuals i, j. Let $F^-(P_1, \ldots, P_n)(X)$ be the group's maximum buying price for a bet on X that pays 1 monetary unit if X is true and 0 otherwise, and $F^+(P_1, \ldots, P_n)(X)$ be the group's minimum selling price for the same bet. Following de Finetti (1974), any probability function Q yields *fair prices* for bets on all $X \in \mathscr{A}$. That is, the maximum buying price for a bet on X is $Q(X)$ and likewise, the minimum selling price for the same bet is $Q(X)$. In other words, $Q(X)$ is a two-sided price for a bet on and against X. Thus, $LP^{\Lambda-}(P_1, \ldots, P_n)(X) = LP^{\Lambda+}(P_1, \ldots, P_n)(X) = LP^{\Lambda}(P_1, \ldots, P_n)(X)$ for all $X \in \mathscr{A}$. Suppose that $P_i(X) < LP^{\Lambda}(P_1, \ldots, P_n)(X) < P_j(X)$. Then, $r_{P_i}^-(LP^{\Lambda}(P_1, \ldots, P_n)(X), X) > 0$, thus violating *No Regrets*. (In this case, we also have $r_{P_j}^+(LP^{\Lambda}(P_1, \ldots, P_n)(X), X) > 0$.)

That completes the list of axioms. Let's wrap up our discussion of them by noting one of the central results in the area, which says that Local Unanimity Preservation and Eventwise Independence together characterize the family of weighted linear pooling strategies (Aczél & Wagner, 1980; McConway, 1981). That is,

Theorem 3 (Aczél & Wagner 1980; McConway 1981). *If F is a pooling strategy and F satisfies Local Unanimity Preservation and Eventwise Independence, then there is a sequence of weights* $\Lambda = (\lambda_1, \ldots, \lambda_n)$ *such that, for any probabilistic credence functions* $P_1, \ldots, P_n$,

$$F(P_1, \ldots, P_n) = LP^{\Lambda}(P_1, \ldots, P_n)$$

Like all characterization results, this one, together with the list of axioms that linear pooling strategies never satisfy, furnishes us with a number of impossibility theorems as corollaries. For instance, there can be no pooling strategy that satisfies Unanimity Preservation, Eventwise Independence, Non-Dictatorship, and External Bayesianity. After all, any one that satisfies the first two axioms is a linear pooling strategy, and the only such strategies that satisfy the fourth axiom are dictatorial and so violate the third axiom.

How concerning is such an impossibility theorem? That depends on how plausible the axioms are. We'll return to Probabilistic Independence Preservation and No Regrets in due course, but let us briefly say why External Bayesianity might not be so desirable.

Daniel and Fang are at a horse race. Each has an unconditional credence for whether Sugar will win the race today, an unconditional credence for whether she won yesterday's race, and conditional credences for whether she will win today given her placing in yesterday's race. Daniel thinks it's very likely she won yesterday, while Fangs think it's very unlikely. Each of them is equally expert on the matter in hand, and so, before they learn about yesterday's race, they should both receive the same weight when we aggregate them to give the group credences. But now they each pick up a newspaper and learn that Sugar won yesterday's race. They both update their credences accordingly. We now ask what weights they should receive when we aggregate their new updated credences to give the group's new updated credences: should we expect them to remain the same as before the evidence came in? A natural answer is that we shouldn't. We should expect Daniel to receive higher weight after the evidence comes in, since he had a much higher credence in the proposition that was learned as evidence – his track record, initially the same as Fang's, is now superior to theirs. If that's right, External Bayesianity is not a feature we should want our pooling strategies to have, for it demands that weights remain the same before and after updating. What's more, the following theorem due to Raiffa (1968) shows that linear pooling actually agrees with our intuitive response to the case of Daniel and Fang:[27]

Theorem 4 (Raiffa 1968). *Suppose that*

(a) P, Q *are probabilistic credence functions defined on* $\mathscr{A}$,
(b) $\Lambda = (\lambda, 1 - \lambda)$ *and* $\Lambda' = (\lambda', 1 - \lambda')$ *are sequences of weights,*
(c) X *and* E *are propositions in* $\mathscr{A}$,
(d) $P(E), Q(E) > 0$,

And suppose that

$$\mathrm{LP}^{\Lambda}(P, Q)(X|E) = \mathrm{LP}^{\Lambda'}(P(-|E), Q(-|E))(X)$$

Then

$$\lambda' = \frac{\lambda P(E)}{\lambda P(E) + (1 - \lambda)Q(E)}$$

---

[27] We give the proof in the Appendix.

and

$$1 - \lambda' = \frac{(1 - \lambda)Q(E)}{\lambda P(E) + (1 - \lambda)Q(E)}$$

That is, if the group's credence before the evidence arrives is a linear pool of the individuals' priors and the group's credence after the evidence is a linear pool of their posteriors, and if the latter is obtained from the former by conditioning on the evidence, then the weight assigned to an individual afterwards is proportional to the weight before and their credence in the evidence.

The upshot: perhaps the failure to satisfy External Bayesianity does not deal a devastating blow against linear pooling. Violating Probabilistic Independence Preservation and No Regrets, however, is less benign, which we'll come to in Section 6.

4.2 Geometric Pooling

Our next collection of pooling strategies belong to the family of multiplicative pooling rules. Unlike the linear pooling strategy that was our concern in the previous section, geometric pooling is defined in two stages.[28] First, we pick a partition of the logical space and pool the credences assigned to the elements of that partition; secondly, we use those pooled credences to define the pooled credences in more coarse-grained propositions.

Let's use Anya, Bon, and Carys again. To specify the geometric pool of their credences, we must specify a partition. So let's take the two-cell partition that contains (i) *Eradicated*, which says polio will be eradicated by 2030, and (ii) *Not Eradicated*, which says it won't. So the epidemiologists' credences are as follows:

	Eradicated	Not Eradicated
Anya	0.2	0.8
Bon	0.6	0.4
Carys	0.7	0.3

As we saw in the previous section, to obtain the linear pool of their credences in *Eradicated*, we simply take their arithmetic mean, that is, $\frac{1}{3}0.2 + \frac{1}{3}0.6 + \frac{1}{3}0.7 = 0.5$, and to obtain the linear pool of their credences in *Not Eradicated*, we take their arithmetic mean as well, that is $\frac{1}{3}0.8 + \frac{1}{3}0.4 + \frac{1}{3}0.3 = 0.5$. And notice that the linear pool of a set of probabilistic credence functions is always guaranteed to be probabilistic itself.

---

[28] Geometric pooling is also known as logarithmic pooling (Genest et al., 1984).

To obtain the geometric pool of their credences in *Eradicated*, we start by taking their geometric mean, that is, $0.2^{\frac{1}{3}} \times 0.6^{\frac{1}{3}} \times 0.7^{\frac{1}{3}} \approx 0.438$. But if we did nothing else and also took the geometric pool of their credences in *Not Eradicated* to be the geometric mean of their credences in that proposition, that is, $0.8^{\frac{1}{3}} \times 0.4^{\frac{1}{3}} \times 0.3^{\frac{1}{3}} \approx 0.458$, we'd end up with non-probabilistic credences, since these two numbers don't sum to 1. So instead of taking the geometric pool of some credences to be their geometric mean, we instead take it to be the normalized geometric mean. That is, we take the geometric means of the credences in each cell of the partition, and then multiply each of these geometric means by the same factor to ensure that the results sum to 1, as credences over a partition are required to do. The pooled credence in any proposition that is a disjunction of elements of the partition is then the sum of the pooled credences in the disjuncts.

Straight Geometric Pooling Suppose:

(i) $P_1, \ldots, P_n$ are probabilistic credence functions defined on $\mathscr{A}$, and
(ii) $\mathscr{S} \subseteq \mathscr{A}$ is a partition.

Then, first: for each S in $\mathscr{S}$,

$$\mathrm{GP}_{\mathscr{S}}(P_1, \ldots, P_n)(S) = \frac{\sqrt[n]{P_1(S) \times \cdots \times P_n(S)}}{\sum_{S' \in \mathscr{S}} \sqrt[n]{P_1(S') \times \cdots \times P_n(S')}}$$

$$= \frac{\prod_{i=1}^{n} P_i(S)^{\frac{1}{n}}}{\sum_{S' \in \mathscr{S}} \prod_{i=1}^{n} P_i(S')^{\frac{1}{n}}}$$

And, second: for any X in $\mathscr{A}$ that is a disjunction of propositions from $\mathscr{S}$,

$$\mathrm{GP}_{\mathscr{S}}(P_1, \ldots, P_n)(X) = \sum_{\substack{S \in \mathscr{S} \\ S \subseteq X}} \mathrm{GP}_{\mathscr{S}}(P_1, \ldots, P_n)(S)$$

One immediate consequence of this definition is that, if we are to pool the credences of a group of individuals who share the agenda $\mathscr{A}$, then there must be a partition $\mathscr{S} \subseteq \mathscr{A}$ such that every proposition in $\mathscr{A}$ is a disjunction of some propositions from this partition. We cannot pool the opinions of a group who have credences only in *The die will land on six, The die will land on an even number, The die will land on a number less than 4*. Of course, this is guaranteed if we assume, as we have done throughout, that $\mathscr{A}$ is the full algebra of subsets of a finite set of possible worlds $\mathscr{W}$.

Another consequence is that the geometric pool of some credences is sensitive to the partition you choose. Suppose Rodrigo and Stefan have the following credences:

	Heavy Rain	Light Rain	No Rain
Rodrigo (P_R)	$1/6$	$1/3$	$1/2$
Stefan (P_S)	$1/3$	$1/6$	$1/2$

Then start with the partition $\mathscr{S} = \{Heavy\ Rain, Light\ Rain, No\ Rain\}$. Then

	Heavy Rain	Light Rain	No Rain
$\text{GP}_{\mathscr{S}}(P_R, P_S)$	0.24	0.24	0.52

Next, the partition $\mathscr{S}' = \{Rain, No\ Rain\}$. Then

	Heavy Rain	Light Rain	No Rain
$\text{GP}_{\mathscr{S}'}(P_R, P_S)$	0.25	0.25	0.5

In fact, just as there is a whole family of linear pooling strategies, each fixed by a sequence of weights, so there is a whole family of geometric pooling strategies:

Geometric Pooling Suppose:

(i) $P_1, \ldots, P_n$ are probabilistic credence functions defined on $\mathscr{A}$,

(ii) $\mathscr{S} \subseteq \mathscr{A}$ is a partition, and

(iii) $\Lambda = (\lambda_1, \ldots, \lambda_n)$ is a sequence of nonnegative real numbers that sum to 1.

Then, first: for each S in $\mathscr{S}$,

$$\text{GP}^{\Lambda}_{\mathscr{S}}(P_1, \ldots, P_n)(S) = \frac{P_1(S)^{\lambda_1} \times \cdots \times P_n(S)^{\lambda_n}}{\sum_{S' \in \mathscr{S}} P_1(S')^{\lambda_1} \times \cdots \times P_n(S')^{\lambda_n}}$$

$$= \frac{\prod_{i=1}^{n} P_i(S)^{\lambda_i}}{\sum_{S' \in \mathscr{S}} \prod_{i=1}^{n} P_i(S')^{\lambda_i}}$$

And, second: for any X in $\mathscr{A}$ that is a disjunction of propositions from $\mathscr{S}$,

$$\text{GP}^{\Lambda}_{\mathscr{S}}(P_1, \ldots, P_n)(X) = \sum_{\substack{S \in \mathscr{S} \\ S \subseteq X}} \text{GP}^{\Lambda}_{\mathscr{S}}(P_1, \ldots, P_n)(S)$$

4.3 Multiplicative Pooling

In fact, even the family of geometric pooling strategies is just one in a larger group of families known as the weighted multiplicative pooling strategies. Where geometric pooling uses sequences of weights that sum to 1, multiplicative pooling strategies use sequences that sum to any positive real number, though the most common is n, where n is the number of individuals pooled. So we have:

Multiplicative Pooling Suppose:

(i) $P_1, \ldots, P_n$ are probabilistic credence functions defined on $\mathscr{A}$,

(ii) $\mathscr{S} \subseteq \mathscr{A}$ is a partition, and

(iii) $\Lambda = (\lambda_1, \ldots, \lambda_n)$ is a sequence of nonnegative real numbers.

Then, first: for each S in $\mathscr{S}$,

$$\mathrm{MP}^\Lambda_{\mathscr{S}}(P_1, \ldots, P_n)(S) = \frac{P_1(S)^{\lambda_1} \times \cdots \times P_n(S)^{\lambda_n}}{\sum_{S' \in \mathscr{S}} P_1(S')^{\lambda_1} \times \cdots \times P_n(S')^{\lambda_n}}$$

$$= \frac{\prod_{i=1}^n P_i(S)^{\lambda_i}}{\sum_{S' \in \mathscr{S}} \prod_{i=1}^n P_i(S')^{\lambda_i}}$$

And, for any X in $\mathscr{A}$ that is a disjunction of propositions from $\mathscr{S}$,

$$\mathrm{MP}^\Lambda_{\mathscr{S}}(P_1, \ldots, P_n)(X) = \sum_{\substack{S \in \mathscr{S} \\ S \subseteq X}} \mathrm{GP}_{\mathscr{S}}(P_1, \ldots, P_n)(S)$$

As we did with linear pooling, let's see which of our axioms geometric and multiplicative pooling strategies satisfy.

(1a) *Local Unanimity Preservation*

No multiplicative pooling strategy satisfies this. Indeed, we saw an example earlier, in which Rodrigo and Stefan both gave credence 0.5 to *No Rain*, but when we pooled over the more fine-grained partition of *Light Rain*, *Heavy Rain*, and *No Rain*, their pooled credence for *No Rain* was 0.52.

(1b) *Global Unanimity Preservation*

Any weighted geometric pooling strategy satisfies this, but no other multiplicative strategy. The problem is that

$$\mathrm{MP}^\Lambda_{\mathscr{S}}(P, \ldots, P)(S) = \frac{P(S)^{\lambda_1 + \cdots + \lambda_n}}{\sum_{S' \in \mathscr{S}} P(S')^{\lambda_1 + \cdots + \lambda_n}}$$

And, if $\lambda_1 + \cdots + \lambda_n \neq 1$, it is easy to find P such that this is not equal to $P(S)$ for all S in $\mathscr{S}$.

(2) *Eventwise Independence*

None of the multiplicative pooling strategies satisfy this. While the numerator in the definition of $\mathrm{MP}^\Lambda_{\mathscr{S}}(P_1, \ldots, P_n)(S)$ depends only on the individuals' credences $P_1(S), \ldots, P_n(S)$ in S, the denominator that normalizes this credence and ensures that the credences in the elements of the partition sum to 1 depends on the individuals' credences in the other elements of the partition.

(3) *Boundedness*

Any pooling strategy that violates Local Unanimity Preservation will violate Boundedness as well. And, in particular, Rodrigo and Stefan's pooled credence in *No Rain* provides an example again. The pooled credence of 0.52 does not lie between the maximum individual credence of 0.5 and the minimum individual credence of 0.5.

(4) *Non-Dictatorship*

As in the case of linear pooling, any multiplicative rule for which $\lambda_i, \lambda_j > 0$ for $i \neq j$ is non-dictatorial.

(5) *External Bayesianity*

Perhaps the most notable feature of the multiplicative rules is that they do satisfy External Bayesianity.

(6) *Probabilistic Independence Preservation*

No non-dictatorial multiplicative rule satisfies this.

(7) *No Regrets*

Like linear pooling, no multiplicative rule satisfies No Regrets. This is made obvious by the multiplicative rules violating Boundedness. Since $\mathrm{GP}^{\Lambda}_{\mathscr{S}}(P_1, \ldots, P_n)(X)$ and $\mathrm{MP}^{\Lambda}_{\mathscr{S}}(P_1, \ldots, P_n)(X)$ can lie outside of $[\min(P_1(X), \ldots, P_n(X)), \max(P_1(X), \ldots, P_n(X))]$ for some $X \in \mathscr{A}$, either $r^-_{P_i}(\mathrm{GP}^{\Lambda}_{\mathscr{S}}(P_1, \ldots, P_n)(X), X) > 0$ or $r^+_{P_i}(\mathrm{GP}^{\Lambda}_{\mathscr{S}}(P_1, \ldots, P_n)(X), X) > 0$ and $r^-_{P_i}(\mathrm{MP}^{\Lambda}_{\mathscr{S}}(P_1, \ldots, P_n)(X), X) > 0$ or $r^+_{P_i}(\mathrm{MP}^{\Lambda}_{\mathscr{S}}(P_1, \ldots, P_n)(X), X) > 0$ for all i. If the group credences lie in $[\min(P_1(X), \ldots, P_n(X)), \max(P_1(X), \ldots, P_n(X))]$ for all $X \in \mathscr{A}$, then the same holds for $\mathrm{GP}^{\Lambda}_{\mathscr{S}}$ and $\mathrm{MP}^{\Lambda}_{\mathscr{S}}$ as LP^{Λ}.

Let's quickly take stock before moving on to imprecise group credences. What has been observed so far is that the linear and multiplicative pooling strategies fail to meet all of the desirable criteria we'd like them to. Take either the entire set of criteria or particular subsets, and we end up with some impossibility results. Notably, the linear and multiplicative rules fare poorly with the pragmatically oriented axioms, Probabilistic Independence Preservation and No Regrets. Given the discussion on group responsibility in Section 2.3, failure to satisfy the latter criteria might hint that it's impossible to provide the sorts of group credences required for an adequate account of collective responsibility. In Section 6, we'll better motivate the axioms and revisit this point.

4.4 Imprecise Probability Pooling

Up until now, we've considered "classical" pooling strategies that map opinion profiles to a single probability function. Rather than mapping sets of credences in propositions to precise, point-valued probabilities, we could pool credences using one of the many tools of *imprecise probability* (IP), giving us sets of probabilities instead, for example, [0.2, 0.7]. On such occasions, we'll use pooling functions taking the form of $\mathscr{F} : \Delta^n_{\mathscr{A}} \to \mathscr{P}(\Delta_{\mathscr{A}})$, where $\mathscr{P}(\Delta_{\mathscr{A}})$ is the power set of $\Delta_{\mathscr{A}}$, which yield sets of probability functions representing the credences of groups.[29]

---

[29] The credences of individuals can be modeled more generally by a (convex or non-convex) set of probability function $\mathbb{P} \subseteq \Delta_{\mathscr{A}}$ and pooled by a function $\mathbb{F} : \mathscr{P}(\Delta_{\mathscr{A}})^n \to \mathscr{P}(\Delta_{\mathscr{A}})$ (see

A group's credences under this account can simply be summarized by a collective *lower probability*

$$\mathscr{F}^-(P_1,\ldots,P_n)(X) = \inf\{P(X) : P \in \mathscr{F}\} \quad \forall X \in \mathscr{A},$$

which induces a collective *upper probability*,

$$\mathscr{F}^+(P_1,\ldots,P_n)(X) = \sup\{P(X) : P \in \mathscr{F}\} \quad \forall X \in \mathscr{A},$$

through a conjugacy relation: $\mathscr{F}^+(P_1,\ldots,P_n)(X) = 1 - \mathscr{F}^-(P_1,\ldots,P_n)(\neg X)$.[30] While $\mathscr{F}^-$ and $\mathscr{F}^+$ may sufficiently summarize a group's credences, they alone don't tell us the whole story. That's why we suggest that IP pooling models also include the set $\mathscr{F}(P_1,\ldots,P_n)$.[31] Throughout, we'll focus on the properties of $\mathscr{F}$. However, that doesn't mean that collective lower probability isn't useful. We'll show that it indeed has an important role. Following the likes of Peter Walley (1991), we give $\mathscr{F}^-$ a behavioral interpretation. Given a bet on X that pays 1 monetary unit if X is true and 0 otherwise for all $X \in \mathscr{A}$, $\mathscr{F}^-(P_1,\ldots,P_n)(X)$ is said to be a group's supremum acceptable buying price for the bet, and $\mathscr{F}^+(P_1,\ldots,P_n)(X)$ the group's infimum acceptable selling price. Thus, the pair $\mathscr{F}^-$ and $\mathscr{F}^+$ have significance under the behavioral interpretation and are central components in the elicitation of group credences in uncertain propositions.

With one *type* of imprecise probability framework at hand that we might exploit in forming group credences,[32] here's a natural candidate for pooling:

Convex Imprecise Probability Pooling Suppose that $P_1,\ldots,P_n$ are probabilistic credence functions defined on the same agenda $\mathscr{A}$.

$$C(P_1,\ldots,P_n) = \text{conv}\{P_i : i = 1,\ldots,n\},$$

where 'conv' is the convex hull operator. Accordingly, C returns the convex hull of credences for all propositions $X \in \mathscr{A}$. (The range of the function is

Stewart & Quintana, 2018, section 7; Elkin, 2021). For the purposes of this Element, however, we stick to *classical profiles*, that is, collections of precise probability functions for $n \geq 2$ individuals, but we acknowledge that the framework could be generalized further to accommodate individually imprecise agents.

30 See e.g., Walley (1991); Bradley (2016); Elkin & Wheeler (2018).

31 For instance, we could have two sets $\mathscr{F}(P_1,\ldots,P_n)$ and $\mathscr{F}^*(P_1,\ldots,P_n)$ that yield the same lower and upper credences for all propositions, yet the sets are structurally different (see Joyce, 2010).

32 The term *imprecise probability* serves as an umbrella for a broad class of models of uncertainty in which sets of probability functions is merely one and among the least general. It covers Dempster-Shafer belief functions (Shafer, 1976), possibility measures (Dubois & Prade, 1988), lower previsions (Walley, 1991), and sets of desirable gambles (Couso & Moral, 2011), among others.

consequently restricted to $\mathscr{D} \subset \mathscr{P}(\Delta_{\mathscr{A}})$, which is the set of all convex sets of probability functions.) The given aggregation rule was considered in the past by Isaac Levi (1985) in forming a consensus between Bayes agents and has been more recently studied systematically by Rush Stewart and Ignacio Ojea Quintana (2018), whose approach we'll often follow.[33]

Some, however, might be curious about the convexity property of the pooling strategy. Convexity, so it seems, is as contentious as how to pool, at least as far as the literature on imprecise probability is concerned. Some see it as a mathematical convenience (e.g., Walley, 1991), while others find it philosophically motivated (e.g., Levi, 1974, 1985; Stewart & Quintana, 2018). Levi (1985), for example, appears somewhat sympathetic to the linear pooling rule as a way of forming a compromise. However, he insists that in case of a disagreement, there is no uniquely rational (linear) compromise that individuals or groups are warranted in adopting. Rather, the set of all possible linear pools must be considered credible, but due to conflict, they are held in suspense. In other words, individuals and groups should *suspend judgment* on all possible credal (linear) compromises. And this commits individuals and groups to adopting the convex hull in their credal judgments provided that all credal distributions are permissible for calculating expectations prior to resolving the conflict through further inquiry.

Of course, not everyone is compelled by Levi's view, but setting aside the philosophical motivations and mathematical considerations, convexity seems quite natural. However, there are practical reasons for why convexity should be abandoned that we'll come to in Section 6. These reasons will also show us why we can't rely solely on lower and upper probabilities. Alternatively, we'll introduce a pooling strategy shortly that relaxes the convexity constraint and that foreshadows the pragmatic concerns convexity gives rise to. But first, let's attend to the given IP pooling strategy and evaluate it under extended versions of our axioms.[34]

(1a) *Local Unanimity Preservation*

If all group members $i = 1, \ldots, n$ have a shared probability function, P, then $C(P_1, \ldots, P_n)(X) = \{P(X)\}$ for all $X \in \mathscr{A}$. Why? Because $\mathrm{conv}\{P\} = \{P\}$.

---

[33] See also Peter Walley's (1982) technical report and Teddy Seidenfeld, Joseph Kadane, and Mark Schervish's (1989) discussion of Levi's proposal situated in decision and social choice theory.

[34] Restatements of some of the axioms that accommodate sets of probabilities are given in Stewart & Quintana (2018) and Elkin (2021). The others are fairly straightforward, and any subtleties that might not be immediately obvious are noted.

(1b) *Global Unanimity Preservation*
This follows from (1a).

(2) *Eventwise Independence*
Here's a sketch. Suppose there's a function $\mathcal{G} : \mathscr{A} \times [0,1]^n \rightarrow \mathscr{P}([0,1])$. Let $\mathcal{G}(X, P_1(X), \ldots, P_n(X)) = \text{conv}\{P_i(X) : i = 1, \ldots, n\}$ for all $X \in \mathscr{A}$. For any $P(X) \in \text{conv}\{P_i(X) : i = 1, \ldots, n\}$, $P(X)$ is some convex combination of $P_i(X)$ for $i = 1, \ldots, n$. Given the definition of C, $C(P_1, \ldots, P_n)(X) = \text{conv}\{P_i(X) : i = 1, \ldots, n\}$ for all $X \in \mathscr{A}$. So, any $P(X) \in C(P_1, \ldots, P_n)(X)$ is some convex combination of $P_i(X)$ for $i = 1, \ldots, n$. It follows that $C(P_1, \ldots, P_n)(X) = \mathcal{G}(X, P_1(X), \ldots, P_n(X))$. $C(P_1, \ldots, P_n)(X)$ thus only depends on the $P_i(X)$'s for all $X \in \mathscr{A}$ and probability functions $P_1, \ldots, P_n$.[35]

(3) *Boundedness*
The IP pooling strategy trivially satisfies Boundedness. Since for all $X \in \mathscr{A}$ and probability functions $P_1, \ldots, P_n$, $\inf C(P_1, \ldots, P_n)(X) = \min(P_1(X), \ldots, P_n(X))$ and $\sup C(P_1, \ldots, P_n)(X) = \max(P_1(X), \ldots, P_n(X))$, $C(P_1, \ldots, P_n)(X) \subseteq [\min(P_1(X), \ldots, P_n(X)), \max(P_1(X), \ldots, P_n(X))]$.[36]

(4) *Non-Dictatorship*
A dictatorship is impossible under C given that necessarily, $P_i \in C(P_1, \ldots, P_n)$ for all $i = 1, \ldots, n$ under all permutations of individuals.

(5) *External Bayesianity*

Proposition 5 (Stewart & Quintana, 2018). *Suppose that $\mathscr{F}$ is a convex IP pooling function, then $\mathscr{F}$ is externally Bayesian.*

A remarkable feature of C is that it's indeed externally Bayesian and it satisfies Boundedness. Recall that linear pooling is the only other strategy satisfying Boundedness, but unfortunately, it's not externally Bayesian. In the classical setup, we have an impossibility result, where no (classical) pooling strategy jointly satisfies Boundedness and External Bayesianity. Although we presented a particular case earlier where External Bayesianity might not be so desirable in our discussion of linear pooling that might mitigate the impossibility result, the property may be necessary in establishing justified group credences (recall Lackey's GEAA account in Section 2.2). The extension to imprecise probabilities affords us an

---

[35] For a more complete but slightly indirect derivation, see the proofs for Lemma 1 and Proposition 2 in Stewart & Quintana (2018).

[36] Note that for imprecise probabilities, Boundedness implies the inclusion rather than the membership of pooled credences.

escape from the impossibility, allowing us to enjoy both properties. The same goes for the combination of Eventwise Independence and External Bayesianity, where only C satisfies both.

(6) *Probabilistic Independence Preservation*

Because C yields the set of all convex combinations of credences for all propositions $X \in \mathcal{A}$ and probability functions $P_1, \ldots, P_n$, C violates Probabilistic Independence Preservation in case $P_i \neq P_j$ for some i, j. Why? Recall Theorem 2 (Laddaga, 1977; Lehrer & Wagner, 1983). A corollary of the theorem is that non-extreme weighted averages of probabilistic credences, for which at least two are not the same, rarely preserve the probabilistic independence of some propositions X and Y that all initially judged to be probabilistically independent. Thus, there exists some $P \in C(P_1, \ldots, P_n)$ such that for propositions X and Y that all i judged to be independent, $P(X|Y) \neq P(X)$.[37]

(7) *No Regrets*

> **Observation 6** (Elkin, 2021). *Suppose that $\mathcal{F}$ is a convex IP pooling function, then $\mathcal{F}$ satisfies No Regrets.*

Elkin (2021) showed in a more general setting, where credences of individuals are modeled as (convex) sets of probability functions, $\mathbb{P}$, that pooling under a convex IP pooling function $\mathcal{F}(\mathbb{P}_1, \ldots, \mathbb{P}_n) = \text{conv}\left(\cup_i \mathbb{P}_i\right)$ entails that no group member has *ex ante* regrets of buying a bet on a proposition X for a price $\mathcal{F}^-(\mathbb{P}_1, \ldots, \mathbb{P}_n)(X)$ nor selling the same bet for a price $\mathcal{F}^+(\mathbb{P}_1, \ldots, \mathbb{P}_n)(X)$ for all individuals $i = 1, \ldots, n$, opinion profiles $(\mathbb{P}_1, \ldots, \mathbb{P}_n)$ in the domain, and propositions $X \in \mathcal{A}$, that is, $r_{\mathbb{P}_i}^-(\mathcal{F}(\mathbb{P}_1, \ldots, \mathbb{P}_n)^-(X), X) = 0$ and $r_{\mathbb{P}_i}^+(\mathcal{F}(\mathbb{P}_1, \ldots, \mathbb{P}_n)^+(X), X) = 0$. Since we're considering classical opinion profiles only, that is, collections of precise probability functions, our convex IP pooling strategy is but a special case – that is, in the more general setting, all $\mathbb{P}_i$ are singleton sets. With C as a special case of the more general IP pooling strategy, it's straightforward to show that no group member has *ex ante* regrets of trading at prices $C^-(P_1, \ldots, P_n)(X)$ and $C^+(P_1, \ldots, P_n)(X)$ for all propositions $X \in \mathcal{A}$.

The convex IP pooling strategy is almost perfect in terms of meeting the desirable criteria we have laid out. Probabilistic Independence Preservation is

---

[37] Although convex IP pooling doesn't satisfy Probabilistic Independence Preservation, Stewart and Quintana (2018) show that it does satisfy a similar constraint, namely, *Confirmational Irrelevance Preservation* (32). We point out that independence is a much richer notion in imprecise probability theory than in classical probability. For an overview of the different concepts, see Cozman (2012).

the only one standing in the way. But notice that none of the other strategies we've considered meet the requirement either, unless if the pooling functions are dictatorial (or in the trivial case of pooling a unanimous opinion profile). Thus, failing to satisfy Probabilistic Independence Preservation might not be all that concerning.

Indeed, Lehrer and Wagner (1983) contend that such a violation is rather benign, as individuals (and groups) are unlikely to have much epistemic interest in the newly established probabilistic dependencies. What Lehrer and Wagner failed to recognize, however, is that such a violation has significant practical implications that individuals and groups will indeed have a significant interest in. We'll come back to this point in Section 6. For now, we want to present an easy fix for imprecise group credences through a weaker rule, although maybe less intuitive:

Non-Convex Imprecise Probability Pooling   Suppose that $P_1, \ldots, P_n$ are probabilistic credence functions defined on the same agenda $\mathscr{A}$.

$$K(P_1, \ldots, P_n) = \{P_i\}_{i=1}^{n}.$$

The upshot of the weaker IP pooling strategy is that we get everything (we leave it to the reader to verify that all the criteria are met). Besides the properties that K enjoys, it has been argued elsewhere that the probabilistic approach as a revisionary method for individual beliefs yields a plausible response to peer disagreement (Elkin & Wheeler, 2018); as a deference principle for policymakers yields a cautious approach to reasoning in the face of scientific disagreement under an epistemic version of the Precautionary Principle (Elkin, 2023); as a non-Bayesian compromise between two Bayes agents with shared preferences can meet the so-called *weak Pareto* criterion; that is, if the two agents strictly prefer a to b, then the compromise position must also reflect the strict preference (Seidenfeld et al., 1989). We'll have more to say about the Pareto criterion later in Section 6.

In addition to the advantages mentioned so far, one might also view K as a middle ground between the equal weight and steadfast views regarding peer disagreement. K encodes equal weight by visibly respecting each credence in an equal manner through their representation in K for all propositions $X \in \mathscr{A}$, which is maintained under all permutations of individuals. At the same time, though, K gives group members a (weak) sense of steadfastness, as the group does not jettison any member's credences in favor of some difference splitting compromise. A closer look at K showcases a reconciliation between two seemingly opposing views. But notice that in whole, K expresses a sort of skepticism through its equal treatment of each $P_i \in K$, ultimately satisfying Feldman and Levi's call for suspended judgment in the face of conflict. In a similar way, C realizes the same benefits, though, in whole, it leans more conciliationist by recognizing and treating credibly every possible difference-splitting compromise by all possible degrees.

Interestingly, what we can take away from Levi's philosophical view of IP as a way of combining credences is that it preserves positive intuitions one might have toward linear pooling since C can be thought of as a mere robustification of LP^Λ. Under such a robustification, C allows us to model ambiguity with respect to the "objectively" correct compromise. That is, ambiguity concerning the objectively correct weighting distribution for individuals $i = 1, \ldots, n$. Taken in a different way, C can be seen as encoding higher-order uncertainty toward the objective linear pool, together with the *principle of indifference*. The function C is thus open to interpretation. Whether one is lured one way or the other is no matter for us. The point is that C offers flexibility in interpreting group credences, all while preserving the intuition that the most feasible compromises are linear pools.

Furthermore, the robustification of linear pooling can be taken in yet another direction. Peter Walley (1991) suggested that IP is not only useful for capturing beliefs and behavior from a more general subjective Bayesian perspective, but it can also be instrumental in confirmatory endeavors in science as an essential tool in robustness or sensitivity analysis. Extended to groups, C (and to some extent K) provides a credible set of compromises for multiple experts. Pick any $P \in C$ as one's prior. Collect some data D and update P on D. Now, update all other possible compromises $Q \in C$. If the confirmatory strength of D is relatively strong for all $Q \in C$, then the confirmatory strength of D is robust with respect to all convex combinations of credences for multiple experts.[38] In other words, even if the weightings of expert opinions wildly differed from that of the chosen P, D would still confer a relatively strong degree of confirmation. Thus, C is not merely the semblance of indeterminacy in this context. Rather, it is a vehicle for furnishing robustness and reassurance as a credible set of compromises representing a group of experts. And the advantage of the External Bayesianity property C and K both possess is that we don't get different outcomes if the order of revisions is changed.

While C and K boast many advantages, both are too inclusive in some instances, making them implausible. With respect to peer disagreement, recall

---

[38] The confirmatory strength of evidence depends on the measure chosen. See Fitelson (1999) for a survey of confirmation measures. But in practice, Bayesians tend to adopt the Bayes Factor (Benjamin et al., 2018). A robust extension of the Bayes Factor is given by Ebner et al. (2019).

Harry from the discussion of the justificationist view. Harry's report that $2 + 2$ does not equal 4 makes his testimony incredible. But in representing you and Harry collectively, his probabilistic credence in the proposition '$2 + 2 = 4$' that is zero (or close to zero) is automatically respected and equally weighed from the group perspective given that it is necessarily in the convex closure of P_{me} and P_{Harry} and the non-convex set $\{P_{me}, P_{Harry}\}$. Or suppose an expert knows that the group is committed to pooling under C or K and that they hold radically unsupported views on the matter. They then submit an extreme credence (close to 1 or 0) contra the overall sentiment of the expert community, biasing the group credence severely in one direction and almost trivializing the collective's attitude, for example, $[0.01, 0.99]$.

What we might say in these kinds of cases is that Harry and the extremist expert ought to be taken less seriously and given little weight, if any at all. Unfortunately for C and K, that's not an option. Some proposals seem to offer some insight into the matter (see, e.g., Nau, 2002), but the optimal solution for IP models is far from certain. And even if a feasible weighting system is established for IP, it's hard to say whether Harry and the extremist expert should be discounted altogether, since by doing so, one must now worry about committing to dictatorial IP pools.

To conclude this section, we sum up the axioms that are met by the introduced pooling strategies on the next page in a final report card featured in Table 1.

5 Promoting Group Epistemic Rationality

In the last section, we asked how well the group credences delivered by the various pooling strategies live up to the demands laid out in Section 3. In this section, we move away from the axiomatic approach and look to evaluate pooling strategies by how well they secure two epistemic ends: accuracy and justification. One may view this section as an attempt at relating pooling and justified group belief (a question that came about in Section 2.2) and how groups might support a commitment to promoting Group Rationality when choosing a pooling strategy.

5.1 Getting to the Truth: How to Measure (In)Accuracy?

We begin with accuracy. The idea is that, while a credence in a proposition can't be true or false in the way that a belief in a proposition can be, it can nonetheless be more or less accurate. For instance, if you are 60% confident it will rain tomorrow, while I'm 5% confident, then we'd likely say that your credence turns out to be more accurate than mine if it does indeed rain, while mine turns out to be more accurate if it doesn't. We begin this section by making

Table 1 Pooling axiom report card

	L-Unanimity Preservation	G-Unanimity Preservation	Eventwise Independence	Non-Dictatorship	Boundedness	External Bayesianity	Probabilistic Independence	No Regrets
LP^Λ	✓	✓	✓	✗	✓	✗	✗	✗
$GP^\Lambda_\mathscr{G}$	✗	✓	✗	✗	✗	✓	✗	✗
$MP^\Lambda_\mathscr{G}$	✗	✗	✗	✗	✗	✓	✗	✗
C	✓	✓	✓	✓	✓	✓	✗	✓
K	✓	✓	✓	✓	✓	✓	✓	✓

clear how we should measure the accuracy of a whole set of credences, rather than just a single one. To do this, we follow an approach often taken in the area of formal epistemology that has come to be known as *accuracy-first epistemology*.[39] There, we say that the *accuracy* of a credence function at a world is its *proximity* to the ideal credence function at that world; and its *in*accuracy is its *distance* from the ideal. So, to specify a measure of accuracy, we must specify the ideal credence function for a given world, and a measure of the distance from one credence function to another. All measures of the inaccuracy of credences agree on which credence function is ideal at a world; they differ in the way they measure distance.

So let's start by identifying the ideal credence function. Suppose $\mathscr{A}$ is the algebra over a finite set of possible worlds $\mathscr{W}$, as introduced in Section 3. We then assume that, for w in $\mathscr{W}$, the credence function defined over $\mathscr{A}$ that best represents w, and hence is most accurate and therefore is ideal, is the one that assigns credence 1 to all propositions in $\mathscr{A}$ that are true at w, and credence 0 to all that are false at w. We write V_w for this credence function; so $V_w(X) = 1$ if X is true at w and $V_w(X) = 0$ if X is false.

Next, the measure of distance from one credence function to another. We needn't go into the mathematical details, but accuracy-first epistemologists tend to assume that we measure these distances using functions known as *additive and continuous Bregman divergences*, and they have a number of arguments for doing so.[40] These are mathematical functions $\mathfrak{D}$ that take two credence functions P and Q defined over the same agenda $\mathscr{A}$ and return a measure $\mathfrak{D}(P,Q)$ of the distance from P to Q. Given such a function $\mathfrak{D}$, we define an inaccuracy measure $\mathfrak{I}$ as follows: the inaccuracy $\mathfrak{I}(P,w)$ of credence function P at world w is $\mathfrak{D}(V_w,P)$.

Here are the two most popular Bregman divergences as illustrations:

- *Squared Euclidean distance*

$$\mathrm{SED}(P,Q) = \sum_{X \in \mathscr{A}} |P(A) - Q(A)|^2$$

- *Generalized Kullback-Leibler divergence*

$$\mathrm{GKL}(P,Q) = \sum_{X \in \mathscr{A}} P(X) \log \frac{P(X)}{Q(X)} - P(X) + Q(X)$$

---

[39] For some representative papers, see Joyce (1998); Greaves & Wallace (2006); Joyce (2009); Leitgeb & Pettigrew (2010a); Leitgeb & Pettigrew (2010b); Pettigrew (2016). See also the Element in this series by Jason Konek and Ben Levinstein.

[40] We'll drop the "additive and continuous" in what follows, since we won't be discussing any other sort of Bregman divergence. For arguments in favour of this way of measuring distance, see Joyce (2009); D'Agostino & Sinigaglia (2010); Pettigrew (2016).

And here are the measures of the inaccuracy of a credence function P at a possible world w that arise from them:

- *Brier score* $\mathfrak{B}(P,w) = \mathrm{SED}(V_w, P)$
- *Additive log score* $\mathfrak{L}(P,w) = \mathrm{GKL}(V_w, P)$

To give a quick illustration, suppose P assigns credence 0.4 to X and 0.6 to its negation. Then its Brier score in the world w in which X is true is:

$$|V_w(X) - P(X)|^2 + |V_w(\neg X) - P(\neg X)|^2$$
$$= |1 - 0.4|^2 + |0 - 0.6|^2 = 0.72$$

One of the attractions of using additive and continuous Bregman divergences for this purpose is that the inaccuracy measures they generate are *additive and continuous strictly proper inaccuracy measures*. We give more details about this class of inaccuracy measures in the Appendix (Section 8), but here we simply note two crucial results we can obtain if we assume that we measure inaccuracy using one of them. These results provide a sort of proof-of-concept for accuracy-first epistemology.

First: Suppose C is a credence function on $\mathscr{A}$ that does not satisfy the probability axioms. Then there is an alternative credence function P on $\mathscr{A}$ that does satisfy those axioms and which is guaranteed to be more accurate than C. That is,

$$\mathfrak{I}(P,w) < \mathfrak{I}(C,w)$$

for all worlds in $\mathscr{W}$. This is due variously to Savage (1971); Joyce (1998); Predd et al. (2009).

Second: Suppose P is a prior probability function on $\mathscr{A}$ and suppose $\mathscr{E} \subseteq \mathscr{A}$ is a partition that contains the possible pieces of evidence you might receive. Suppose R is an updating rule that takes each possible piece of evidence E in $\mathscr{E}$, and returns a posterior probability function R_E, which it recommends as the correct response to learning E. Let the inaccuracy of R at world w be the inaccuracy of the posterior it recommends when you learn the piece of evidence that is true at w. Then R minimizes expected inaccuracy from the point of view of the prior P if R recommends updating by Bayes' Rule: that is, $R_E(X) = P(X \mid E)$ whenever $P(E) > 0$. This result is due to Greaves & Wallace (2006).

In what follows, we will always assume that the inaccuracy of a credence function at a world is given by an additive, continuous, and strictly proper measure.

5.1.1 The Accuracy of Pooling Strategies I

With this account of the accuracy of a credence function, we can now ask how well a pooling strategy performs by this standard. How accurate are the credences to which it gives rise?[41]

The community of Shakespeare scholars is huge. Nonetheless, let's assume that we have asked each of them how likely they think it is that various historical individuals – Christopher Marlowe, Francis Bacon, Edward de Vere, Shakespeare himself – were the author of the works traditionally attributed to William Shakespeare of Stratford-upon-Avon. Now we wish to summarize their views, perhaps because we are writing an article on the state of the debate. We pick a pooling strategy and apply it to the individual credences. It gives us a credence function we might ascribe to the scholarly community. Now suppose that credence function has the following feature: there's another one that we might have ascribed to the scholarly community but didn't, and every member of the scholarly community thinks that alternative one would be more accurate; that is, from the point of view of each individual's own personal credence function, that one is better than the one we actually ascribed, in expectation. In that sort of situation, it seems that we've ascribed the wrong credences to the group. So we should demand that this situation doesn't occur. Here is a formal statement of the property we'd like our pooling strategy F to have:

Accuracy Consensus. Suppose $\mathfrak{I}$ is an additive and continuous strictly proper inaccuracy measure. For any sequence of individual credence functions $P_1, \ldots, P_n$, defined on $\mathscr{A}$, if $Q = F(P_1, \ldots, P_n)$, then there should be no group credence function $Q^\star$ defined on $\mathscr{A}$ such that, for all P_i,

$$\mathbb{E}_{P_i}(\mathfrak{I}(Q^\star)) = \sum_{w \in \mathscr{W}} P_i(w)\mathfrak{I}(Q^\star, w) < \sum_{w \in \mathscr{W}} P_i(w)\mathfrak{I}(Q, w) = \mathbb{E}_{P_i}(\mathfrak{I}(Q))$$

Now, it turns out that this is sufficient to narrow the field of pooling strategies to just the linear ones. That is, Accuracy Consensus characterizes the linear pooling strategies.[42]

---

[41] This question also holds a central place in a broader field of study called *the wisdom of crowds*. Assessing the accuracy of judgments in collective settings (de Condorcet, 1785) and quantities more generally (Galton, 1907) has a long tradition. When it comes to binary outcomes, however, the linear pool tends to provide neutral judgments closer to 0.5 when opinions are diverse. More recently, some have suggested that in improving on the accuracy, pooled credences should be *extremized*, that is, pushed closer to 0 or 1, under mathematical transformation (Ranjan & Gneiting, 2010; Baron et al., 2014; Satopää et al., 2014). This is a fascinating literature, and we encourage the reader to investigate it further, but unfortunately, a proper discussion can't be given in the limited space afforded here.

[42] We give the proof in the Appendix.

Theorem 7 (Pettigrew, 2019b). *Suppose $\mathfrak{I}$ is an additive and continuous strictly proper inaccuracy measure. Then:*

(i) *If there is no sequence of weights $\Lambda = (\lambda_1, \ldots, \lambda_n)$ such that $Q = \mathrm{LP}^\Lambda$ $(P_1, \ldots, P_n)$, then there is an alternative credence function $Q^\star$ such that, for each P_i,*

$$\mathbb{E}_{P_i}(\mathfrak{I}(Q^\star)) = \sum_{w \in \mathcal{W}} P_i(w)\mathfrak{I}(Q^\star, w) < \sum_{w \in \mathcal{W}} P_i(w)\mathfrak{I}(Q, w) = \mathbb{E}_{P_i}(\mathfrak{I}(Q))$$

(ii) *If there is a sequence of weights $\Lambda = (\lambda_1, \ldots, \lambda_n)$ such that $Q = \mathrm{LP}^\Lambda$ $(P_1, \ldots, P_n)$, then there is no alternative credence function $Q^\star$ such that, for each P_i,*

$$\mathbb{E}_{P_i}(\mathfrak{I}(Q^\star)) = \sum_{w \in \mathcal{W}} P_i(w)\mathfrak{I}(Q^\star, w) < \sum_{w \in \mathcal{W}} P_i(w)\mathfrak{I}(Q, w) = \mathbb{E}_{P_i}(\mathfrak{I}(Q))$$

We want our pooling strategy to satisfy Accuracy Consensus in cases in which it is important that all the individuals in the group can get behind the group credence we have ascribed to them collectively. So this is not so important when we're asking how an individual should respond in a case of peer disagreement – in those cases, it really doesn't matter whether the peers with which you disagree can get behind your new credences, since they're your credences alone and not theirs. But it is important if you are representing the group's opinions to others, such as in the dispute over the authorship of *Hamlet*, or if you are using the group's credence to assess whether the group is liable for some harm their collective action has caused, such as in the corporate liability case we considered earlier.

In these cases, if accuracy is the goal of our precise credences, we have an argument in favor of linear pooling. But what if accuracy is also the goal of our imprecise credences? Does this favor a particular way of pooling these opinions? This is an open question. So far, there is no fully satisfactory theory of credal accuracy for imprecise credences. The major stumbling block is a suite of impossibility results that show there can be no way to measure the accuracy of imprecise credences that has a property analogous to the strict propriety of measures like the Brier score or the logarithmic scoring rule for their precise counterparts (Seidenfeld et al., 2012; Mayo-Wilson & Wheeler, 2016; Schoenfield, 2017). For any putative measure, there must be imprecise credences that think of themselves as worse than some alternative. Nonetheless, hope is not lost. Jason Konek (2019) has proposed a strategy for solving the problem, though the technical details remain to be worked out. It might be hoped that, once this is done, we can formulate an argument for a particular way of pooling imprecise credences.

For the moment, however, we might point out some interesting implications of Theorem 7 relating to imprecise credences. It says that, for some probabilistic credence functions $P_1, \ldots P_n$, the convex hull, that is, conv$\{P_i : i = 1, \ldots, n\}$, is the set of all and only those credence functions that are not dominated in expected accuracy relative to $P_1, \ldots, P_n$; that is, all and only those credence functions for which there is no alternative preferred in expectation by all members of the group. Interestingly, this is exactly the set that the IP pooling function C returns when it's asked to pool $P_1, \ldots, P_n$. Might this furnish us with an accuracy-based argument for that pooling function? It certainly suggests an argument against any IP pooling function that returns a set that includes probability functions that conv$\{P_i : i = 1, \ldots, n\}$ does not include: those functions will be dominated in expectation. It's less obvious that it can provide an argument against an IP pooling function that returns a set that does not include members that conv$\{P_i : i = 1, \ldots, n\}$ does include. Accuracy considerations are good at ruling out credence functions that lie outside the convex hull, but they don't say anything particularly positive about those that lie inside, beyond saying that they aren't ruled out.

5.1.2 The Accuracy of Pooling Strategies II

Let's put aside imprecise credences for now. Here's another accuracy-based consideration in favor of linear pooling. So far, we've been considering only how to aggregate individuals' credences. But, for many of the pooling strategies available, we can use them to aggregate any attitude that is represented numerically. For instance, we might use them to aggregate estimates of numerical quantities, such as estimates of the price of fuel in 2024, or the average height of a 41-year-old French person in 1872, or the first year in the future in which humans no longer exist. And if we consider these quantities and these estimates, we might measure their accuracy using the squared Euclidean distance between the estimate and the true value, just as we measured the accuracy of a credence earlier using the squared Euclidean distance between it and the credence that best represents the world.

Lila, Mona, and Nomy are at their local county fair, where there's a competition to estimate the weight of the prize marrow in kilograms. Lila says 100, Mona says 94, and Nomy say 93. In fact, it's 91. Francis, who is running the competition, notices that the average inaccuracy of the three estimates is greater than the inaccuracy of the straight linear pool of those estimates. That is,

$$\frac{1}{3}(100 - 91)^2 + \frac{1}{3}(94 - 91)^2 + \frac{1}{3}(93 - 91)^2 > \left(\frac{100 + 94 + 93}{3} - 91 \right)^2$$

After a quick calculation, he concludes that this is no coincidence. However many quantities they were estimating, whatever the true values had been, and whatever estimates they gave, providing they were not all the same, it would have been the case that, had you to choose between using the straight linear pool of their estimates or picking one of them at random and using that person's estimates, the linear pool would have been more accurate in expectation. This is a corollary of a result that is sometimes known as the Diversity Prediction Theorem (Galton, 1907; Page, 2007). Here's the theorem:[43]

Theorem 8 (Page, 2007). *Suppose $(X_1, \ldots, X_m)$ is a sequence of quantities, whose true values are given by the sequence $T = (t_1, \ldots, t_m)$. For each individual i, $A_i = (a_{i1}, \ldots, a_{im})$ gives their estimates of the quantities. Then*

$$\text{SED}\left(T, \frac{1}{n}\sum_{i=1}^{n} A_i\right) = \frac{1}{n}\sum_{i=1}^{n}\text{SED}(T, A_i) - \frac{1}{n}\sum_{i=1}^{n}\text{SED}\left(A_i, \frac{1}{n}\sum_{i=1}^{n} A_i\right)$$

And here's the corollary:

Corollary 9. *Suppose $(X_1, \ldots, X_m)$ is a sequence of quantities, whose true values are given by the sequence $T = (t_1, \ldots, t_m)$. For each individual i, $A_i = (a_{i1}, \ldots, a_{im})$ gives their estimates of the quantities. Then, if $A_i \neq A_j$ for some i, j, then*

$$\text{SED}\left(T, \frac{1}{n}\sum_{i=1}^{n} A_i\right) < \frac{1}{n}\sum_{i=1}^{n}\text{SED}(T, A_i)$$

Perhaps you find this an attractive feature of linear pooling. Do any other strategies boast this property too? As the following theorem shows, they do not.[44]

Theorem 10. *Suppose $X_1, \ldots, X_m$ is a sequence of quantities. For each individual i, $A_i = (a_{i1}, \ldots, a_{im})$ gives their estimates of the quantities. Now suppose that $A \neq \sum_{i=1}^{n}\frac{1}{n}A_i$. Then there are possible true values $T = (t_1, \ldots, t_m)$ of the quantities such that*

$$\text{SED}(T, A) > \frac{1}{n}\sum_{i=1}^{n}\text{SED}(T, A_i)$$

This accuracy-based argument for linear pooling becomes relevant when you are pooling the credences of a group of individuals in order to set your own credences, and you wish to do so in a way that is as accurate as possible. Perhaps you work in local government and you're charged with forming an opinion on the consequences of a proposed housing project, a topic about which you have no expertise whatsoever. You call up a variety of experts and ask their opinions. They all have different credences in the relevant propositions – perhaps not wildly different, but certainly not exactly the same. How should you set your credences? You could pick one of the experts at random and defer to them; or you could pool the individuals' credences and defer to that. Straight linear pooling guarantees that the second option is more accurate in expectation; and it is the only pooling operator that does. This might tell in favor of using linear pooling.

Interestingly, in just the sort of case where the Diversity Prediction Theorem seems to tell in favor of linear pooling, there is a result that tells against it. In these situations, it seems that you would demand the following: were you to learn the opinion of only one expert, you should just defer to that; were you to learn the opinion of two experts, you should defer to the pool of their opinions. But there's something else we should want as well. We've assumed that you yourself don't have any opinions about the topic in question – that's why you're asking the experts! So you presumably don't have any credences about what the experts will say either, nor what your conditional credences are on the topic given what the experts say. Nonetheless, you should at least want it to be possible to fill in those credences, both conditional and unconditional, in such a way that your deference to the experts individually and to the pool of their opinions would be the result of updating using Bayes' Rule on what you've learned about their opinions. And you should want that to be possible even if you think the experts might disagree – indeed, you should want it to be possible especially in those cases! More formally, here's the condition you want, where E_1 is the random variable that gives the credence of the first expert in proposition X, E_2 is the random variable that gives the credence of the second expert in X, and we say that you defer to E_i if, upon learning only the probability that E_i assigns to X, you'd set your credence in X to match it.

Deference Compatibility. There is a probability function P such that

(i) $P(E_1 = E_2) < 1$. That is, it thinks it's possible that E_1 and E_2 differ in their opinion about X.

(ii) $P(X \mid E_1 = p) = p$ and $P(X \mid E_2 = q) = q$. That is, P defers to each of the two experts individually.

(iii) $P(X \mid E_1 = p, E_2 = q) = F(p, q)$. That is, P defers to the pool of the two experts.

A number of researchers have noticed that linear pooling doesn't satisfy Deference Compatibility (Dawid et al., 1995; Bradley, 2018; Gallow, 2018;

Dawid & Mortera, 2020).[45] And, more recently, Snow Zhang has shown that a large range of other pooling functions doesn't do it either (Zhang, ms).

So our local government official, tasked with forming their own opinion on the basis of the opinions of the experts they've consulted, faces something of a dilemma. Linear pooling gives him the benefits of the Diversity Prediction Theorem, but falls foul of Deference Compatibility.

5.1.3 The Principle of Coherent Minimal Mutilation

So far, we've been using squared Euclidean distance and the other Bregman divergences to measure the distance from the true values of a series of quantities to a series of estimates of those quantities, or from the most accurate credences in a series of propositions to a series of other credences in those propositions. But there is another use to which we might put them. This is inspired by the work of Konieczny and Pino Pérez (1998, 1999) on the topic of merging operators, which take different sources of information that might conflict with one another and try to extract a single coherent source.[46]

Oskar, Prince, and Quentin are the senior executives of a corporation that is being sued for some misdemeanor. At the heart of the case is the question of whether the company believed that their actions would cause the harms they did in fact cause. We know the credences of each of the executives, but we need to identify credences for the executive team itself. It's natural to think that, in order to do that, we need to identify credences to which the three executives, and more importantly their lawyer, could not object.

Here's one sort of grounds on which they might object: they might say that the credences assigned to the executive team, or the corporation more broadly, lie further from their individual credences than is necessary. Of course they recognize that, since the three of them have different credences, whatever is ascribed to the group will divergence from the opinions of at least two of them. But they might reasonably demand that the group credences diverge as little as is necessary from their own. Here's one way of making this precise: first, pick a measure of the distance between credence functions; second, say that a group's credence function is the credence function such that the sum of the distances from it to each of the individuals' credence functions is minimal. Here's a formal version – it has a distance measure $\mathfrak{D}$ as a parameter, so that there are different versions depending on how you measure that distance.

---

[45] We give the proof in the Appendix.

[46] For other work in this tradition, see Osherson & Vardi (2006); Pigozzi (2006); Predd et al. (2008).

Principle of Coherent Minimal Mutilation$_{\mathfrak{D}}$. If $P_1, \ldots, P_n$ are probability functions on $\mathscr{A}$, then

$$\text{CMM}_{\mathfrak{D}}(P_1, \ldots, P_n) = \min_{P \in \Delta_{\mathscr{A}}} \sum_{i=1}^{n} \mathfrak{D}(P, P_i)$$

where $\Delta_{\mathscr{A}}$ is the set of probability functions over $\mathscr{A}$.

Osherson & Vardi (2006) and Predd et al. (2008) call this the Coherent Approximation Principle. It turns out that, if we measure the distance using the squared Euclidean distance measure, this principle characterizes the linear pooling strategy.

Theorem 11 (Osherson & Vardi, 2006). *If $P_1, \ldots, P_n$ are probability functions on $\mathscr{A}$, then*

$$\text{LP}(P_1, \ldots, P_n) = \text{CMM}_{\text{SED}}(P_1, \ldots, P_n) = \min_{P \in \Delta_{\mathscr{A}}} \sum_{i=1}^{n} \text{SED}(P, P_i)$$

However, as mentioned earlier, squared Euclidean distance is just one of many legitimate ways to measure the distance from one credence function to another. Another one is the generalized Kullback-Leibler function. And if we apply the Principle of Coherent Minimal Mutilation with that, we obtain geometric pooling (Pettigrew, 2019a).

Theorem 12 (Pettigrew, 2019a). *If $P_1, \ldots, P_n$ are probability functions defined on $\mathscr{A}$, then*

$$\text{GP}_{\mathscr{G}}(P_1, \ldots, P_n) = \text{CMM}_{\text{GKL}}(P_1, \ldots, P_n) = \min_{P \in \Delta_{\mathscr{A}}} \sum_{i=1}^{n} \text{GKL}(P, P_i)$$

When should we pool using the Principle of Minimal Mutilation? Perhaps in the same cases in which we should abide by Accuracy Consensus, that is, when it is important that the individuals in the group can get behind the group opinion that we ascribe to them. There is a contractualist flavor to both approaches. The idea is that it is legitimate to ascribe an attitude to a group if the members do not have reason to complain about the ascription. They would have reason to complain about the ascription if there were an alternative one that each of them expects to be more accurate; and they would have reason to complain if there were an alternative whose total distance from the individual opinions is less.

5.2 Revisiting Justified Group Belief

Often, we would like our pooling functions to preserve whatever justification the individual members of a group have for assigning the credences they do, as suggested in Section 2. So, if each individual in a group is justified in assigning the credences she does, you might hope that the credences you assign to the group on the basis of your pooling function are also justified. What might we mean by this, and how might we hope to achieve it? Here's one condition that captures some of what we might want and that seemingly aligns with Lackey's GEAA view discussed in Section 2.2: If each member of the group begins with the same prior credences and then updates those on their own private evidence, then pooling the individuals' posterior credences should get you to the same probability function as updating the shared prior probability function on the conjunction of the individuals' evidence. After all, if the shared prior is the unique justified prior probability function, then posterior credences are justified just in case they are obtained from that prior by updating on the available evidence. So the individuals are justified just in case their credences are the shared priors updated on their private evidence, and the group is justified just in case its credences are the shared priors updated on the group's evidence, which is the conjunction of the private evidence of its members. Here's this requirement more formally:

Evidence Pooling. For all probability functions $P_1, \ldots, P_n$ on $\mathscr{A}$ and all propositions $E_1, \ldots, E_n$ in $\mathscr{A}$, if each individual i assigns positive probability to E_i, so that $P_1(E_1), \ldots, P_n(E_n) > 0$, then, for all propositions X in $\mathscr{A}$,

$$F(P_1(-\mid E_1), \ldots, P_n(-\mid E_n))(X) = F(P_1, \ldots, P_n)(X \mid E_1 \wedge \ldots \wedge E_n)$$

Notice that this differs from External Bayesianity by allowing that different individuals can receive different evidence. External Bayesianity is therefore a special case.

Now it turns out that two of the pooling functions we've met so far boast this property: if we use any weighted geometric pooling or weighted multiplicative pooling operator over the most fine-grained partition – that is, the partition given by the possible worlds – then they satisfy Evidence Pooling (Baccelli & Stewart, 2023; Weisberg & Pettigrew, 2023).[47]

However, it's not clear how useful such a pooling function is in this context.[48] After all, suppose we wish to use it to extract and pool the evidence

---

[47] We give the proof in the Appendix.

[48] The discussion that follows in the remainder of this section borrows from Winkler (1968); Morris (1983); Weisberg & Pettigrew (2023).

from the individuals in the group. Then, we have to collect, for each individual, the credences they assign to every element in the most fine-grained partition, namely, the one given by the possible worlds. And if we must do that, it would have been easier just to ask each individual for their private evidence, and then update the shared prior on that. The pooling function is overkill.

This raises an interesting question. In many cases within science, we're interested in a sequence of hypotheses, which form a partition, while the evidence any given scientist might gather forms a different partition, and neither of these partitions is a fine- or coarse-graining of the other. Often, in such situations, each hypothesis assigns a chance to each of the different possible pieces of evidence, and this allows us to use Bayes' Theorem (together with the Principal Principle) to update our priors to given our posteriors when we learn a particular piece of evidence.[49] In physics, the hypotheses might be different theories of the behavior of subatomic particles and the different possible pieces of evidence might be different outcomes of an experiment we're about to run; in climate science, the hypotheses might be different versions of a single model that are obtained by specifying different values for a particular parameter, such as climate sensitivity, and the evidence might be readings transmitted from a radiosonde.

If $H_1, \ldots, H_k$ is a partition of hypotheses, and E is a piece of evidence, and H_i says that the chance of E is $C_i(E)$, then Bayes' Theorem (together with the Principal Principle) says:

$$P(H_i|E) = \frac{P(H_i)P(E|H_i)}{\sum_{j=1}^{k} P(H_j)P(E|H_j)} = \frac{P(H_i)C_i(E)}{\sum_{j=1}^{k} P(H_j)C_j(E)}$$

For instance, suppose I am holding a coin, and each hypothesis H_i posits a different bias q_i for the coin. The coin is then tossed N times and lands heads M times. Hypothesis H_i assigns probability $q_i^M(1 - q_i)^{N-M}$ to this evidence. So the posterior credence upon learning it is

$$P(H_i|E) = \frac{P(H_i)q_i^M(1 - q_i)^{N-M}}{\sum_{j=1}^{k} P(H_j)q_j^M(1 - q_j)^{N-M}}$$

Now suppose Taj has prior P_1, while Ursula has P_2. They then witness different sequences of coin tosses. Taj witnesses N_1 tosses with M_1 heads among them; we'll call this evidence E_1. Ursula witnesses N_2 tosses with M_2 heads among

---

[49] The Principal Principle is a constraint on your credences. It says that your credence in a proposition, conditional on the objective chance of that proposition being r, should be r. That is, $P(X \mid \text{chance of } X \text{ is } r) = r$.

them; we'll call this E_2. And now suppose we apply geometric pooling to their posteriors over the partition $H_1, \ldots, H_n$, which we'll call $\mathcal{H}$:[50]

$$\mathrm{GP}_{\mathcal{H}}(P_1(-|M_1 \text{ out of } N_1), P_2(-|M_2 \text{ out of } N_2))(H_i)$$
$$= K\left(P_1(H_i)q_i^{M_1}(1-q_i)^{N_1-M_1}\right)^{\frac{1}{2}} \left(P_2(H_i)q_i^{M_2}(1-q_i)^{N_2-M_2}\right)^{\frac{1}{2}}$$
$$= \mathrm{GP}_{\mathcal{H}}(P_1, P_2)(H_i | {}^{1}/_{2}(M_1 + M_2) \text{ out of } {}^{1}/_{2}(N_1 + N_2))$$

That is, aggregating the posteriors of our individuals using geometric pooling gives the same result we'd get if we were to aggregate their priors and then update not on their total evidence but their total evidence with the sample size halved. If Taj saw 20 heads out 100 tosses and Ursula saw 80 out of 200, geometrically pooling their posteriors would give the same result as pooling their priors and updating them on seeing 50 heads out of 150, rather than 100 heads out of 300. And of course, since geometric pooling satisfies Unanimity Preservation, if Taj and Ursula have the same prior, the geometric pool of their posteriors will be that shared prior updated on their evidence with the sample size halved.

We can avoid the problem of halving the sample size by moving from geometric pooling to multiplicative pooling.

$$\mathrm{MP}_{\mathcal{H}}(P_1(-|M_1 \text{ out of } N_1), P_2(-|M_2 \text{ out of } N_2))(H_i)$$
$$= K\left(P_1(H_i)q_i^{M_1}(1-q_i)^{N_1-M_1}\right) \left(P_2(H_i)q_i^{M_2}(1-q_i)^{N_2-M_2}\right)$$
$$= \mathrm{MP}_{\mathcal{H}}(P_1, P_2)(H_i | (M_1 + M_2) \text{ out of } (N_1 + N_2))$$

The problem is that multiplicative pooling doesn't satisfy Unanimity Preservation. So, even if Taj and Ursula share the same prior, the multiplicative pool of their posteriors will not be their shared prior updated on their total evidence with the full sample size.

Finally, notice that this fact about multiplicative pooling is not peculiar to cases of coin tosses and hypotheses that specify Bernoulli distributions. Suppose that each hypothesis H_i specifies a chance function C_i, and suppose that possible pieces of evidence E and F are probabilistically independent according to each C_i – that is, $C_i(E \,\&\, F) = C_i(E)C_i(F)$. Then

$$\mathrm{MP}_{\mathcal{H}}(P(-|E), Q(-|F)(H_i)$$
$$= K(P(H_i)C_i(E)) \, (Q(H_i)C_i(F))$$
$$= KP(H_i)Q(H_i)C_i(E \,\&\, F)$$
$$= \mathrm{MP}_{\mathcal{H}}(P, Q)(H_i | E \,\&\, F)$$

50 In what follows, K is a normalizing constant.

So, in sum, multiplicative pooling is the best pooling operator we have met if we hope to assign group credences that inherit the justification of the individual credences they pool.

6 Promoting Group Practical Rationality

As individuals and as groups, credences play two roles in our lives. They record how we represent the world to be and they guide our actions. This is why we said Group Rationality in Section 2.2 should be extended to include practical goals of groups also. In the previous section, we asked which pooling strategies give us group credences that are instrumental in meeting some fundamental epistemic aims concerning accuracy and justification. In this section, we ask which furnish us with group credences that serve as good guides to action and further promote Group Rationality. Specifically, we want a pooling strategy to give us group credences that are the most effective means to achieving practical goals, thereby making good on the commitment to the ideal ethos, extended to practical rationality. We'll see that some pooling strategies fail to live up to the standard through induced consequences that are contrary to any rational group's practical interests, leaving groups liable for the group credences formed under such strategies.[51]

But before we get to those issues, let's first jog the reader's memory on the basics of expected utility theory that is taken as the standard for rational behavior.

6.1 A Quick Primer on Expected Utility Theory

We'll present Savage's (1954) version of expected utility theory here, since it is the most straightforward, but everything we'll say in this section holds for other formulations of the theory as well.

A decision problem consists of:

(i) a set $\mathcal{O}$ of different options that are available to the person who faces it, and
(ii) a set $\mathcal{S}$ of states of the world for which the outcomes of the various options in $\mathcal{O}$ are defined, where $\mathcal{S}$ is a partition.

Savage's version of expected utility theory requires an individual who faces a decision problem to have:

---

[51] Recall from Section 2.3 on group responsibility that groups can be held liable for the intentional attitudes they hold, including their credences. The responsibility is passed down to all the members regardless of their role given their complicity through a joint commitment to the group's ethos.

(a) a probabilistic credence function P that takes each state S in $\mathscr{S}$ and gives the individual's credence $P(S)$ in that state, and

(b) a utility function U that takes each option A in $\mathscr{O}$ and each state S in $\mathscr{S}$ and gives the utility $U(A,S)$ that the individual assigns to choosing A in S.

We then define the expected utility of each option A in $\mathscr{O}$ from the point of view of P as follows:

$$\mathbb{E}_P(U(A)) = \sum_{S\in\mathscr{S}} P(S)U(A,S)$$

Expected utility theory then requires us to choose an option that has maximal expected utility.

6.2 Dutch Booking Newly Established Dependencies

As suggested at the start of the section, we ideally want pooling strategies to guide us in making good decisions, and to do so in accordance with expected utility theory. Like with a pooling strategy's epistemic viability, its pragmatic viability might be indicated through its properties. Let's focus then on the pragmatically oriented axiomatic constraints on pooling strategies introduced in Section 3.

The first we'll consider is the Probabilistic Independence Preservation axiom. Recall that it says that if all individuals $i = 1,\ldots,n$ judge $X, Y \in \mathscr{A}$ to be probabilistically independent, that is, $P_i(X|Y) = P_i(X)$, then the pooled credences for X and Y should maintain this independence property. Why? Consider Bill and Sue whose credences concerning the outcome of a biased coin toss with an unknown bias are given as follows.

	Heads	Tails
Bill (P_B)	$1/4$	$3/4$
Sue (P_S)	$3/5$	$2/5$

In addition to those credences, Bill and Sue are both opinionated on a separate matter, namely, the weather today.

	Rain	$\neg$ Rain
Bill (P_B)	$7/10$	$3/10$
Sue (P_S)	$2/5$	$3/5$

Although Bill and Sue have different credences in the possible outcomes in these two matters, both agree that they're probabilistically uncorrelated. That is, $P_B(Rain \wedge Heads) = P_B(Rain)P_B(Heads)$, $P_S(\neg Rain \wedge Tails) = P_S(\neg Rain)P_S(Tails)$, and so on.

Suppose now that Bill and Sue agree to pool their credences to come up with group credences that they may employ jointly if they were to bet on the propositions. For convenience, let's say that Bill and Sue choose the Straight Linear Pooling strategy. The following provides a summary, where the first two columns are the credences of Bill and Sue and the last two columns the straight linear pools of their credences.

	$P_B(\cdot \wedge \cdot)$	$P_S(\cdot \wedge \cdot)$	$LP(\cdot \wedge \cdot)$	$LP(\cdot)\,LP(\cdot)$
Heads $\wedge$ *Rain*	0.175	0.24	0.2075	0.23375
Tails $\wedge$ *Rain*	0.525	0.16	0.3425	0.31625
Heads $\wedge \neg$ *Rain*	0.075	0.36	0.2175	0.19125
Tails $\wedge \neg$ *Rain*	0.225	0.24	0.2325	0.25875

Unfortunately for Bill and Sue, maintaining that the two matters under consideration remain probabilistically uncorrelated after pooling puts them in a bad situation. Suppose that a clever bookie has observed Bill and Sue's pooling strategy. The bookie now has a strong incentive to propose to Bill and Sue one of many combinations of bets on the conjunctions of propositions. Here is one such combination that Bill and Sue should see as fair. The bookie will buy for $207.50 Bet 1 from Bill and Sue that pays $1000 if *Heads* $\wedge$ *Rain* is true and nothing otherwise. The bookie will buy for $316.25 Bet 2 from Bill and Sue that pays $1000 if *Tails* $\wedge$ *Rain* is true and nothing otherwise. The bookie will buy for $191.25 Bet 3 from Bill and Sue that pays $1000 if *Heads* $\wedge \neg Rain$ is true and nothing otherwise. The bookie will buy for $232.50 Bet 4 from Bill and Sue that pays $1000 if *Tails* $\wedge \neg Rain$ is true and nothing otherwise.[52]

Bets 1-4 book a sure loss for Bill and Sue, despite Bill and Sue expecting the bundle to break even on both sides. How so? We know that the bookie can obtain a reward of $1000 at most since only one of the conjunctive propositions can be true. Given that the set of bets exhausts all possibilities, the bookie is guaranteed to win one of the bets. Bill and Sue aimed to ensure that the outcome is a wash by charging the bookie a price in line with the probabilistic group credences for each bet yielded by LP. Where they go wrong, though, is in maintaining that the two matters under consideration remain probabilistically uncorrelated, that is, $P(\cdot \wedge \cdot) = P(\cdot)P(\cdot)$. The bookie recognized that Bill and Sue's pooling strategy does not preserve probabilistic independence and exploited their compromise by swapping the value given by $LP(\cdot)LP(\cdot)$ with $LP(\cdot \wedge \cdot)$ in Bets 2 and 3, which Bill and Sue remained committed to being the same. As a result, the bookie's expected utility from the four bets is $52.50,

---

[52] For convenience, we'll assume throughout that utility is linear in money.

whereas Bill and Sue's is –$52.50. Whatever the case may be, Bill and Sue are sure to surrender the latter amount.[53]

Did Bill and Sue have bad judgment in this particular instance? Not necessarily. It's quite sensible for them individually and as a group to judge that a coin toss is irrelevant to whether it rains or not before and after pooling their credences. But that is just what Probabilistic Independence Preservation says. Considering the practical irrationality we have seen that emerges when the axiom is flouted by pooling strategies, it seems that the Probabilistic Independence Preservation is an axiom worth satisfying. Indeed, we might be further compelled by it upon connecting the consequences of violating Probabilistic Independence Preservation with an earlier discussion from Section 2.3. If group members are complicit qua intentional participants in actions performed by the group, then Probabilistic Independence Preservation seems like a desirable constraint all members would be jointly committed to upholding. For they are all liable for bad outcomes resulting from a chosen strategy that violates it. In this instance, Bill and Sue are responsible for the unnecessary loss resulting from their chosen pooling strategy.

By holding groups liable for their decisions, including deciding on a pooling strategy for forming group credences, choosing a pooling strategy is further constrained. The trouble is that most of the pooling strategies we've seen fare poorly when it comes to living up to this group responsibility. Recall that linear, geometric, multiplicative, and convex IP pooling all violate Probabilistic Independence Preservation.[54] Only the non-convex IP function is able to meet the demand.

Perhaps what we might conclude from this discussion is that in purely epistemic terms, Lehrer and Wagner may be right that the violation is benign. But susceptibility to a Dutch Book, as shown earlier, is a nontrivial concern, as no pooling strategy should commit groups to booking a sure loss. Not only would that be irresponsible toward the group agent but all the members individually, given that they all individually safeguarded themselves by having probabilistic credences, yet by merely forming a betting coalition, they now are jointly susceptible to being Dutch Booked. The pragmatic implications of the axiom discussed here provide further support for the axiom, despite only one pooling strategy satisfying it.

---

[53] Our Dutch Book argument is a variation of those given by Kyburg & Pittarelli (1996) and Elkin & Wheeler (2018).

[54] We remind the reader that independence is a more nuanced concept in IP.

6.3 No Regrets, or How to Stop Throwing Away Money

The No Regrets axiom similarly aims at avoiding unnecessary loss if a group were to make bets on uncertain propositions. The difference, however, is that No Regrets concerns *ex ante* loss whereas Probabilistic Independence Preservation concerns *ex post* loss (although the loss is knowable before resolving the decision-maker's uncertainty).[55] Whether one of the resulting feelings is worse than the other is an empirical matter, but we take for granted that both are undesirable. In this section, we'll try to better motivate No Regrets and show its plausibility.

As many know, used car salesmen thrive on swindling unknowing and often innocent customers. The lessons of George Akerlof's (1970) seminal paper highlight the significance of *information asymmetry* and how it can be exploited in these kinds of markets. Used car dealerships seemed to have taken notice and apparently have settled on charging hefty premiums for their vehicles whether in good shape or bad. Unfortunately for the average consumer, the information asymmetry puts them at a disadvantage not only in buying a quality car but also in bargaining. While not every buyer having to transact with a dealer deserves sympathy, it seems fair to commend those who do their best in the face of information asymmetry. That is, those who do their best at mitigating their exposure to surrendering an excess amount of money through an exchange for a perceptibly overpriced asset or forfeiting a fair price by selling an asset for less than its perceived value.

Consider Lisa and Stan who are jointly in the market for a used car with a $10,000 budget each has equally contributed to. They have collected information on a class of cars that suit their needs and some basic red flags that might be present. After perusing a car lot, Stan spots a car he is familiar with. Overall, it looks like the car is in good condition and has a moderate amount of mileage on it. Stan is willing to pay the sticker price of $9,999. Asking for Lisa's opinion, Stan learns that she's very much pessimistic that this would be a reasonable deal. In fact, Lisa reveals that her estimate is much lower and she would only pay $6,000. While they both like the car, they are at a stalemate on price and ultimately its value.

Suppose that Lisa lets Stan dictate, leading him to buy the car at the asking price. They both feel relieved by the car seeming to run well. But setting aside the car's condition over the long-term, was the purchase itself a good deal for both of them? As it turns out, not so much. After taking the car out for a spin,

---

[55] The *ex ante* aspect also differentiates it from Loomes and Sugden's (1982) more general *regret theory* that attends to *ex post* regret, but the motivation is not all that different from theirs as well as more recent accounts of regret aversion (Arntzenius, 2008; Arvan, 2020).

they meet a friend who is a knowledgeable appraiser at a leading appraisal firm. Hating that she has to be the bearer of bad news, the friend informs them at the current valuation, the car is worth at most $6,000. It turns out that Lisa was on to something. Both immediately feel significant regret toward the price they jointly paid for the car. Like many others, they too got swindled by the infamous used car salesman. The thought of overpaying that much for the vehicle sickens them both.

Suppose instead of Lisa letting Stan dictate, the two agree to compromise. Stan is willing to come down on the offer as long as Lisa is willing to come up. That is to say that the compromise is in the *bounds*, exclusively, of their buying prices. Lisa, still reluctant to play along due to *expecting any price paid higher than $6,000 to incur a loss from her perspective*, agrees for the sake of the group. Stan makes an offer of $8,000 to the dealer. After some showboating hesitation, the dealer accepts with unexpressed rejoice. Unfortunately for Lisa and Stan, the story concludes in the same way. While they saved a noninsignificant amount of money this time around, paying 33% above the car's valuation still is not in their best interest. Again, it appears that Lisa was on to something all along.

What lesson can we draw from this classic and maybe all too familiar tale? For one thing, collectively exchanging money for goods engenders a risk of unnecessary loss resulting from paying too much. Of course, we can reconstruct the case to show that on the other side, the risk of selling an asset for too little can be just as salient and the regret also being psychologically painful if realized.[56] A feasible principle would suggest that as these risks present themselves, groups are wise to minimize them. That is just what No Regrets says in the context of trading bets. Treating the credences of all group members as pricing signals on bets, a group should *suspend judgment* on the set of all prices in-between the bounds in the face of conflict and only transact at the prices where there is agreement.

Recall Levi's view from Section 4.4. That means that for all $X \in \mathscr{A}$, the group should happily buy a bet for a price x as high as $\min(P_1(X), \ldots, P_n(X))$ since all prices $x \leq \min(P_1(X), \ldots, P_n(X))$ are acceptable by $i = 1, \ldots, n$ and sell the bet for a price y as low as $\max(P_1(X), \ldots, P_n(X))$ since all prices $y \geq \max(P_1(X), \ldots, P_n(X))$ are acceptable by $i = 1, \ldots, n$. Any price in (x, y) will give at least one i *ex ante* regret of transacting, and from the group's perspective, that signal should be taken as a forewarning of an increased risk of overpaying or underselling the bet if the group were to pool in a way that ignores i's signal.

---

[56] Whether the intensity of regret varies on the different sides of transactions is an empirical matter.

If the group proceeds to pool in a way that ignores such a signal, the group is liable for any bad deals made.[57]

One final thing we'll mention on the No Regrets axiom is that while it might not entail that groups maximize expected utility at the group-level in accordance with the demands of Savage's theory, one can still view it as a principle of practical rationality for *ambiguity averse* groups.[58] For each individual i in the group, i's expectation of buying a bet on $X \in \mathscr{A}$ for a price $u \in [0, \infty)$ is

$$P_i(X)(1 - u) + (1 - P_i(X))(-u)$$

Every $u > P_i(X)$ implies that the expectation is negative and thus $r_{P_i}^-(u, X) > 0$. No Regrets ensures that individually, no member's expectation for paying a price u given by a pooling function is negative, thus minimizing the *ex ante* regret of overpaying for the bet. The axiom commits a group then to taking a cautious approach when choosing a maximum buying price $u \in [0, \infty)$, letting $\min(P_1(X), \ldots, P_n(X))$ determine it on the group's behalf for all $X \in \mathscr{A}$, as the group has a nonnegative expectation for buying a bet at a price u and thus no *ex ante* regrets for any i when $u = \min(P_1(X), \ldots, P_n(X))$. We leave it to the reader to see how this similarly follows for a *selling* price $v \in [0, \infty)$ when $v = \max(P_1(X), \ldots, P_n(X))$.

6.4 The Ex Ante Pareto Condition

The practical irrationality resulting from violating the Probabilistic Independence Preservation and No Regrets axioms narrowly focuses on betting behavior. But groups are likely to have practical interests in things beyond betting. As we said before, group credences should serve as a good guide to action. In this section, we consider a principle concerned more generally with group decision-making called *Ex Ante Pareto*. To motivate it, consider the following example.

Gail, Harb, and Isamu are effective altruists. Each is a total hedonic utilitarian, so they all share the same utility function, which values an outcome in accordance with how much pleasure it contains and how little pain. They all have different credence functions. As a group, they'd like to provide a list

---

[57] A quick note on pooling strategies that don't satisfy Boundedness. When it comes to placing bets, the group will be happy on one side, depending on the side of the interval $[\min(P_1(X), \ldots, P_n(X)), \max(P_1(X), \ldots, P_n(X))]$ that $F(P_1, \ldots, P_n)(X)$ lands on, but all $i = 1, \ldots, n$ will be unhappy on the opposite transactional side since they all will have *ex ante* regrets. If $F(P_1, \ldots, P_n)(X) \in [\min(P_1(X), \ldots, P_n(X)), \max(P_1(X), \ldots, P_n(X))]$, then the same holds for multiplicative pooling strategies as the linear pooling strategies.

[58] See Gilboa & Schmeidler (1989) for an axiomatization of ambiguity averse preferences. Ambiguity averse agents tend to abide by the so-called Γ-Maximin decision criterion. See Seidenfeld (2004) for a discussion of the decision rule, which we'll come back to shortly.

of charities that they take to offer the greatest expected goodness per dollar donated. So they seek a strategy by which to pool their credences, which they'll then combine with their shared utility function using expected utility theory in order to give an assessment of the various possible charities they might list. Which strategy should they choose?

When they're making their list, they naturally want to avoid a situation in which there are two options, A and B, such that each individual expects A to be better than B, but the group's credences expect B to be better than A. In fact, the inconsistency wouldn't only be odd, but potentially unjustified if individually, the members *jointly accept* that A is better than B in expectation, yet the group expects the reverse. To avoid such an outcome, it's reasonably straightforward to see that, if they use a linear pooling strategy, they'll avoid this for sure. After all, given a single utility function and multiple credence functions, the expected utility of an option by the lights of a linear pool of the credence functions is just a weighted average of the expectations of that option from the point of view of the individual credence functions. That is,

$$\mathbb{E}_{\lambda_1 P_1 + \cdots + \lambda_n P_n}(U(A)) = \lambda_1 \mathbb{E}_{P_1}(U(A)) + \cdots + \lambda_n \mathbb{E}_{P_n}(U(A))$$

So, if $\mathbb{E}_{P_i}(U(A)) > \mathbb{E}_{P_i}(U(B))$, for all i, then

$$\mathbb{E}_{\lambda_1 P_1 + \cdots + \lambda_n P_n}(U(A)) > \mathbb{E}_{\lambda_1 P_1 + \cdots + \lambda_n P_n}(U(B))$$

In the jargon, we say that linear pooling strategies satisfy the *Ex Ante* Pareto condition.

> ***Ex Ante* Pareto** For any probabilistic credence functions $P_1, \ldots, P_n$, any utility function U, and any options A and B, if, for all i, $\mathbb{E}_{P_i}(U(A)) < \mathbb{E}_{P_i}(U(B))$, then $\mathbb{E}_{F(P_1, \ldots, P_n)}(U(A)) < \mathbb{E}_{F(P_1, \ldots, P_n)}(U(B))$.

What's more, the linear pooling strategies are the only (classical) ones that satisfy it. Here is the corollary of a theorem due to Philippe Mongin (1995) that shows this:[59]

Theorem 13 (Mongin, 1995). *Suppose U is a utility function. And suppose F is a pooling strategy that is not a linear pooling strategy. Then there are credence functions* $P_1, \ldots, P_n$ *and options A and B such that*

(i) $\mathbb{E}_{P_i}(U(A)) > \mathbb{E}_{P_i}(U(B))$, *for each i, and*
(ii) $\mathbb{E}_{F(P_1, \ldots, P_n)}(U(A)) < \mathbb{E}_{F(P_1, \ldots, P_n)}(U(B))$.

In the example that motivated this discussion, we assumed that our three effective altruists agree on their utility function. But what about a case in which the

---

[59] We give a proof in the Appendix.

individuals whose opinion we wish to aggregate disagree on both credences and utilities? Consider Jasper and Kamal who are trying to decide whether to stay at home or go to the cinema to see a new film called *Ocean*. However, neither is sure whether the film is a nature documentary or a casino heist. They have different utilities for those two options, as well as different credences concerning which it is:

Credences	Nature	Heist		Utilities	Nature	Heist
Jasper	$3/4$	$1/4$		Jasper	3	−5
Kamal	$1/4$	$3/4$		Kamal	−5	3

As a result, both Jasper and Kamal assign an expected utility of 1 to going to see *Ocean*, though for different reasons. And let's assume that both agree that staying at home will have a utility of 0 for sure, and so an expected utility of 0 for both of them. Then they both prefer the cinema to staying at home. But suppose we now ask what they would choose to do as a group. We use linear pooling to combine their credences, giving a group credence of $1/2$ that *Ocean* is a nature documentary and $1/2$ that it is a heist movie. But then notice this: whether we use Jasper's utility function or Kamal's or some weighted average of the two, it turns out that the expected utility of going to the cinema will be −1, while the expected utility of staying at home remains 0. Although they both prefer the cinema to staying at home, the group they comprise prefers staying at home to going to the cinema. So, while linear pooling assures us of the *Ex Ante* Pareto property when the members of the group have the same utility function, it does not when they have different ones. And, due to a classic result by Mongin (1995), no pooling strategy does. But Mongin's result is situated in the traditional setup that doesn't allow for IP pooling rules. So, how do such strategies fare in satisfying the Pareto criterion?

Before trying to answer this question, we note that expected utility with imprecise probabilities is more nuanced than the classical theory, although the latter can be recovered as a special case. This is because there are various ways to evaluate options, given that we're now considering sets of expected utilities for each option produced under a non-empty (convex or non-convex) set of probability functions. That said, here are just a couple of ways. On the weaker side,

Maximality. For a non-empty (convex or non-convex) set of probability functions, $\mathbb{P}$, utility function, U, and options $A, B \in \mathcal{O}$, A is (strictly) preferred to B iff for all $P \in \mathbb{P}$, $\mathbb{E}_P(U(B)) < \mathbb{E}_P(U(A))$; A is said to be admissible iff for all $B \in \mathcal{O}$, there exists some $P \in \mathbb{P}$ such that $\mathbb{E}_P(U(B)) \leq \mathbb{E}_P(U(A))$.[60]

---

[60] See Walley (1991).

We might think of the set, $\mathbb{P}$, here as a *credal committee*, where each $P \in \mathbb{P}$ is a committee member (Joyce, 2010). Under this personification, Maximality implies that for any $A \in \mathcal{O}$, A is inadmissible iff all of the committee members of the credal committee are in agreement that A is expected to be strictly worse than some other option B. Quite naturally, Maximality extends classical expected utility theory by credal committees and yields a robust decision criterion.

On the cautious side, we've already come across the Γ-Maximin decision criterion in our discussion of No Regrets (footnote 58). To put it succinctly,

> Γ-Maximin. For any non-empty (convex or non-convex) set of probability functions, $\mathbb{P}$, utility function U, and options $A, B \in \mathcal{O}$, A is (strictly) preferred to B iff $\underline{\mathbb{E}}(U(B)) < \underline{\mathbb{E}}(U(A))$, where $\underline{\mathbb{E}}(U(\cdot)) = \min\{\mathbb{E}_P(U(\cdot)) : P \in \mathbb{P}\}$ is the *lower expected utility* for all options; A is said to be admissible iff for all $B \in \mathcal{O}$, $\underline{\mathbb{E}}(U(B)) \leq \underline{\mathbb{E}}(U(A))$.

The latter tells us to consider the worst-case expected utilities for all options and take the best of worst. While the criterion is naturally pessimistic, it's often associated with decisions made in the face of ambiguity (Gilboa & Schmeidler, 1989).

From the given IP-based decision criteria, we may draw some plausible restatements of the *Ex Ante* Pareto condition:

> ***Ex Ante* Pareto** $_{Maximality}$ For any probabilistic credence functions $P_1, \ldots, P_n$, any utility function U, and any options A and B, if, for all i, $\mathbb{E}_{P_i}(U(A)) < \mathbb{E}_{P_i}(U(B))$, then for all $P \in \mathcal{F}(P_1, \ldots, P_n)$, $\mathbb{E}_P(U(A)) < \mathbb{E}_P(U(B))$.

and

> ***Ex Ante* Pareto** $_{\Gamma-Maximin}$ For any probabilistic credence functions $P_1, \ldots, P_n$, any utility function U, and any options A and B, if, for all i, $\mathbb{E}_{P_i}(U(A)) < \mathbb{E}_{P_i}(U(B))$, then $\underline{\mathbb{E}}_{\mathcal{F}(P_1, \ldots, P_n)}(U(A)) < \underline{\mathbb{E}}_{\mathcal{F}(P_1, \ldots, P_n)}(U(B))$.

It's obvious that our non-convex strategy K satisfies ***Ex Ante* Pareto** $_{Maximality}$. Why? K just is the set of probability functions for $i = 1, \ldots, n$. So, the strict inequality holds with respect to all the expectations given by all $P_i \in$ K if the strict inequality holds with respect to the expectations of all i individually. But what about the convex strategy C? What we obtain from the results of Mongin (1995) is that given any sequence of nonnegative weights $\lambda_1, \ldots, \lambda_n$ such that $\sum_{i=1}^n \lambda_i = 1$ and probability functions $P_1, \ldots, P_n$, any convex combination of the probability functions and corresponding weights, $\lambda_1 P_1 + \cdots + \lambda_n P_n$, satisfies *Ex Ante* **Pareto** (assuming a shared utility function U). Since every $Q \in C(P_1, \ldots, P_n)$ is a convex combination of $P_1, \ldots, P_n$, Q satisfies *Ex Ante* **Pareto** with a fixed U if $\mathbb{E}_{P_i}(U(A)) < \mathbb{E}_{P_i}(U(B))$ for $i = 1, \ldots, n$. Thus, C satisfies *Ex Ante* **Pareto** $_{Maximality}$ with a fixed U if $\mathbb{E}_{P_i}(U(A)) < \mathbb{E}_{P_i}(U(B))$ for $i = 1, \ldots, n$. But just the same as in the linear pooling case, the Pareto condition is violated if individuals disagree on utilities for both C and K (Seidenfeld et al., 1989).

Suppose instead that a group is more cautious and bases their evaluation of the options in $\mathscr{O}$ on Γ-Maximin. We can straightforwardly show that functions C and K satisfy *Ex Ante* **Pareto** $_{\Gamma-Maximin}$. Assume that $\mathbb{E}_{P_i}(A) < \mathbb{E}_{P_i}(B)$ for $i = 1, \ldots, n$. Let $\mathscr{E}(U(A)) = \{\mathbb{E}_P(U(A)) : P \in C(P_1, \ldots, P_n)\}$ and $\mathscr{E}(U(B)) = \{\mathbb{E}_P(U(B)) : P \in C(P_1, \ldots, P_n)\}$ be the set of expectations given under $C(P_1, \ldots, P_n)$ for A and B, respectively. In case all P_i are identical, $\mathscr{E}(U(A))$ and $\mathscr{E}(U(B))$ are singleton sets, and it is not the case that $\mathbb{E}_{P_i}(U(A)) \geq \mathbb{E}_{P_i}(U(B))$ for P_i by our initial assumption. So, $\min \mathscr{E}(U(A)) < \min \mathscr{E}(U(B))$. Now, assume instead that $P_j \neq P_k$ for some j, k. Let P_j yield the $\min \mathscr{E}(U(B))$. We already know that $\mathbb{E}_{P_j}(U(A)) < \mathbb{E}_{P_j}(U(B))$ by assumption. And by definition, $\min \mathscr{E}(U(A)) \leq \mathbb{E}_{P_j}(U(A))$. It follows that $\min \mathscr{E}(U(A)) < \min \mathscr{E}(U(B))$. This suffices to show that $C(P_1, \ldots, P_n)$ satisfies *Ex Ante* **Pareto** $_{\Gamma-Maximin}$. The same applies for $K(P_1, \ldots, P_n)$.

Again, these results hold only if there is some utility function, U, shared by $i = 1, \ldots, n$. While such a limitation might make the results seem less important, there are times when a common utility function may be held by a group for expediency, for example, in determining public policy. But in general, the limitation can't be ignored since values often differ among individuals and consequently, individuals will have different utility functions (recall Jasper and Kamal). Supposing that Jasper and Kamal are Bayes agents, there is only one solution for them that preserves Pareto. As Seidenfeld et al. (1989) showed for two Bayes agents with different utility functions and different probability functions, the set of probability and utility function pairs for the Bayes agents is the only solution that satisfies the Pareto requirement (see point (i) in Theorem 1 of their paper).

6.5 The Instability of Group Preferences

Violations of *Ex Ante* Pareto raise another problem for groups who wish to act on their pooled credences. As noted earlier, when we use decision theory to help us make a choice that we face, we render that choice as a decision problem, complete with options and states of the world. But to do this we must decide at which level of grain to describe the states of the world. For instance, suppose you are trying to decide whether to take an umbrella when you leave the house. You might describe the decision problem using just two states of the world: *Rain* and *No rain*. Or you might choose a slightly finer grained description: *Heavy rain, Light rain, No rain*. Or an even more fine-grained description: *Heavy rain for the first hour and light rain thereafter*; *Light rain throughout*; *Light rain for the first hour and heavy rain thereafter*; *Heavy rain throughout*; *No rain*. And so on. A key assumption in much standard individual decision theory is that it shouldn't matter which level you choose. That is, you should never find yourself in a situation where you prefer to take the umbrella when the problem is stated at one level of grain, while you prefer to leave it behind when it is stated at another level.[61] This is assured in various versions of expected utility theory by assuming that the utility you assign to a coarse-grained outcome is just your expectation of its utility in terms of any set of more fine-grained outcomes that make it up.[62] So, for instance, the utility you assign to taking an umbrella when it rains is the utility you assign to taking an umbrella in heavy rain, weighted by your credence in heavy rain given it rains at all and you take an umbrella, plus the utility you assign to taking an umbrella in light rain, weighted by your credence in light rain given it rains at all and you take an umbrella. We might call such an assumption *Inter-Grain Coherence*.

But what the example of the cinema goers shows is that we cannot guarantee this in the case of group decision-making. If we describe the decision so that there is just one state of the world, and the group must choose between going to the cinema and staying at home, the group will prefer to go to the cinema, since it has utility 1 in that single state of the world, while staying home has utility 0. But if we describe it so that there are two states of the world, one in which *Ocean* is a nature documentary and the other in which it is about a casino heist, the group will prefer to stay at home, since the pooled credences will favor doing that, regardless of whose utility function we use. Indeed, as Matthias Hild (2001) shows, it is possible to describe cases in which there is a long chain of finer and finer grained descriptions of a decision problem, together with assignments of utilities and credences to them, such that the group's preferences, calculated by pooling both credences and utilities using linear pooling, flip back and forth as you move from level to level. What's more, this isn't just a problem for linear pooling. It follows from any violation of the *Ex Ante* Pareto property. And, as Mongin's theorem showed, any pooling strategy whatsoever violates that. So, if you wish to make decisions using the credences you obtain

---

[61] In decision theory, this is known as *the problem of partition invariance* or *partition sensitivity*. See, for instance, (Weirich, 2020, Section 3.2).

[62] See, for instance, Joyce (1999, 176–178).

from your pooling strategy, you can't be confident that, had you elicited the individuals' credences and utilities at a finer level of grain, and pooled those, you wouldn't have ordered the options differently. And that undermines the normative force of the ordering that you in fact have.

Now there's a natural response to this problem in theory. For any group of individuals, we can describe the states of the world at such a level of grain that everything that any member of that group cares about is specified within the descriptions of the states of the world. At this point, any further fine-graining adds no detail that changes the individuals' utilities. And so no further fine-graining can lead to flips of preference. We might then propose always to use that level of grain when we aggregate the opinions of the individuals to give the group preference ordering.

The problem with this proposal is that it isn't feasible. Think of the myriad things that affect the utility you assign to a situation: the number of drops of rain that fall on you when you're out without an umbrella, their temperature, their size, the duration of the rain shower, the water-resistance of your footwear, the likelihood of a car driving through a nearby puddle and splashing you; and that's before we even look outside the immediate situation to consider the precise well-being of those you care about, the future state of the environment, and so on. Inter-Grain Coherence is so important precisely because we want to be sure that the level of grain at which we choose to describe the states of the world in our decision problem does not matter because we can only feasibly use decision theory to guide our actions if we can approach the decision using a fairly coarse-grained set of states of the world. But for group decision-making based on pooled credences, it isn't available.

In closing this section, perhaps the take home message is that when it comes to group decision-making, respecting some ideal pragmatic constraints under pooled credences is quite difficult to achieve. We illustrated what happens when Probabilistic Independence Preservation and No Regrets are flouted. And we considered another feasible constraint, namely, *Ex Ante* Pareto, and showed why it's a further feature we would want pooling strategies to meet, but again, it's another one that's hard to meet without some strict assumptions.

As per Section 2.3, groups can be held liable for failing to live up to the expectations of preventing the undesirable outcomes we described in this section. Given that few pooling strategies satisfy Probabilistic Independence Preservation and No Regrets and that none satisfy *Ex Ante* Pareto when utility functions differ, what we might come to realize is that it's impossible for groups to live up to all their responsibilities when acting under pooled credences. We signaled so much after discussing the multiplicative strategies in Section 4 and have made it apparent here.

Some, however, might suggest that the constraints we've considered on group decision-making are too stringent, but we contend that no viable interpretation of Group Rationality, taken as part of a group's ethos, would ever admit to such consequences being acceptable. This leaves us in a bit of an awkward position, as pooling should benefit groups in their practical endeavors, but considering the picture painted here, things look fairly grim.

7 Relaxing Some Constraints

So far, we have made two important idealizing assumptions. First, we've assumed that every individual in the group has the same agenda – that is, they assign credences to exactly the same propositions. Second, we've assumed that every individual in the group has coherent credences – that is, their credence function is probabilistic. In the wild, these assumptions fail more often than they hold. How might we aggregate opinions in the cases in which they fail? We'll ask first how to aggregate incoherent agents and then ask how to aggregate individuals with different agendas.

7.1 Aggregating Incoherent Individuals

One decision we must make from the outset: should we require that the credence function given by our pooling strategy is itself coherent, even if the individuals' credence functions are not? How we answer this depends on the use to which we wish to put that strategy. If we will use it to provide a summary of the individuals' beliefs, there is no need to require this. For instance, if Veronica and Wei both have high credences in a proposition and also both have high credences in its negation, and are thereby incoherent, then it seems that a summary of their credences should also give a high credence to the proposition and a high credence to its negation, and so should be incoherent itself. On the other hand, if we will use the pooled credences to make a decision, then it seems we must ensure that they are coherent, since all of our decision theories require coherent credences as inputs.[63] We'll describe both approaches here.

Little has been written on this question, and in this section, we will follow the lead of one of the few existing proposals. We met it already in Section 5.1.3. It was first proposed in this context by Osherson and Vardi (2006), and developed further by Predd et al. (2008) and Pettigrew (2019a).

Begin by fixing an agenda $\mathscr{A}$. We'll assume throughout this section that all individuals have this same agenda. Suppose we have a function that measures

---

[63] For instance, see our presentation of Savage's version of expected utility theory in the last section.

how far one credence function lies from another when both are defined on this agenda. Call the measure $\mathfrak{D}$. Earlier, we met two examples of such measures: the squared Euclidean distance, and the generalized Kullback-Leibler divergence. Importantly, those measure distance from any credence function to any another, regardless of whether either or both are probabilistic. Now, given a profile of credence functions $C_1, \ldots, C_n$, each of which may or may not be probabilistic, we say that the pool of these functions is the credence function C such that the sum of the distances from C to each of the C_is is minimal. That is:

Principle of Minimal Mutilation$_\mathfrak{D}$

$$MM_\mathfrak{D}(C_1, \ldots, C_n) = \arg \min_C \sum_{i=1}^{n} \mathfrak{D}(C, C_i)$$

Earlier, we saw two results:

(i) if we take $\mathfrak{D}$ to be the squared Euclidean distance measure, and the individual credence functions are probabilistic, and we demand that the pooled credence function is too, then the resulting pooling strategy is just linear pooling;

(ii) if we take $\mathfrak{D}$ to be the generalized Kullback-Leibler divergence, and the individual credence functions are probabilistic, and we demand that the pooled credence function is too, then the resulting pooling strategy is just geometric pooling.

It turns out that, if we do not require that the individual or pooled credences are probabilistic, we obtain the following:

(ii) if we take $\mathfrak{D}$ to be the squared Euclidean distance measure, the pooled credence function is just the linear pool of the individual credence functions; that is,

$$MM_{SED}(C_1, \ldots, C_n)(X) = \frac{1}{n}C_1(X) + \cdots + \frac{1}{n}C_n(X)$$

(ii) if we take $\mathfrak{D}$ to be the generalized Kullback-Leibler divergence, the pooled credence function is not the geometric pool of the individual credence functions, as you might expect; rather, the pooled credence in each element of the partition is the geometric mean of the individual credences in that element; that is,

$$MM_{GKL}(C_1, \ldots, C_n)(S) = C_1(S)^{\frac{1}{n}} \times \cdots \times C_n(S)^{\frac{1}{n}}$$

But now let's suppose that we do want the pooled credences to be probabilistic. Then there seem to be three routes we might take.

(i) We might simply say that the pool of $C_1, \ldots, C_n$ is the *probabilistic* credence function C such that the sum of the distances from C to each of the C_is is minimal. This is just the Principle of Coherent Minimal Mutilation that we met earlier.

$$\mathrm{CMM}_{\mathfrak{D}}(C_1, \ldots, C_n) = \underset{P \in \Delta_{\mathscr{A}}}{\arg\,\min} \sum_{i=1}^{n} \mathfrak{D}(P, C_i)$$

(ii) Or we might first apply the Principle of Minimal Mutilation $\mathrm{MM}_{\mathfrak{D}}$ and then afterwards fix up any incoherence in the resulting pooled credence function. And indeed, there's a natural way to do that using our distance measure $\mathfrak{D}$: if C is incoherent, we fix it up by taking the probabilistic credence function P for which the distance from P to C is minimal. That is,

$$\mathrm{Fix}_{\mathfrak{D}}(C) = \underset{P \in \Delta_{\mathscr{A}}}{\arg\,\min}\, \mathfrak{D}(P, C)$$

So, on this proposal, we aggregate possibly incoherent credences as follows:[64]

$$(\mathrm{Fix}_{\mathfrak{D}} \circ \mathrm{MM}_{\mathfrak{D}})(C_1, \ldots, C_n) = \mathrm{Fix}_{\mathfrak{D}}(\mathrm{MM}_{\mathfrak{D}}(C_1, \ldots, C_n))$$

(iii) And, finally, we first fix up the incoherent individual credences first, and then apply our standard pooling strategies to this.

$$(\mathrm{MM}_{\mathfrak{D}} \circ \mathrm{Fix}_{\mathfrak{D}})(C_1, \ldots, C_n) = \mathrm{MM}_{\mathfrak{D}}(\mathrm{Fix}_{\mathfrak{D}}(C_1), \ldots, \mathrm{Fix}_{\mathfrak{D}}(C_n))$$

So there are three options: pool-then-fix, fix-then-pool, fix-and-pool-together.

We might hope that these three routes to aggregation agree with one another. It turns out that, if we focus only on groups whose shared agenda is a partition, then using generalized Kullback-Leibler to aggregate credences and fix up incoherences does lead to three methods that always agree; however, if we use squared Euclidean distance instead, and the partition has more than two cells, we don't (Pettigrew, 2019a). Then:

Theorem 14 (Pettigrew, 2019a).

(i) $\mathrm{CMM}_{\mathrm{SED}} = \mathrm{Fix}_{\mathrm{SED}} \circ \mathrm{MM}_{\mathrm{SED}} \neq \mathrm{MM}_{\mathrm{SED}} \circ \mathrm{Fix}_{\mathrm{SED}}$

(ii) $\mathrm{CMM}_{\mathrm{GKL}} = \mathrm{Fix}_{\mathrm{GKL}} \circ \mathrm{MM}_{\mathrm{SED}} = \mathrm{MM}_{\mathrm{GKL}} \circ \mathrm{Fix}_{\mathrm{GKL}}$

What can we conclude from this result? It might provide the foundations for a "no dilemma" argument in favor of using generalized Kullback-Leibler

---

[64] Here, we use the mathematical notation $\circ$. If f and g are functions, then $f \circ g$ is the function that results from first applying g and then applying f. It is sometimes read as 'f following g'. So, for instance, if f and g are both one-place functions, $(f \circ g)(x) = f(g(x))$.

divergence instead of squared Euclidean distance to measure distance between credence function, and therefore geometric pooling instead of linear pooling to aggregate credences. After all, if you use squared Euclidean distance, you must decide whether you will aggregate a set of incoherent credence functions and then fix them up so that they are coherent, or whether you should first fix them up and then aggregate them. The theorem shows that these give different results. And it seems there's no nonarbitrary way to decide which to use. If you use generalized Kullback-Leibler, on the other hand, you avoid this dilemma.

7.2 Aggregating Individuals with Different Agendas

Xia and Yoaav are climate scientists who study future sea level rise. Xia assigns credences to two propositions: sea level will rise by less than 1cm in the next ten years, which we'll call X; sea level will rise by between 1 cm and 2 cm in the next ten years, which we'll call Y. Yoaav also assigns credence to two propositions: he doesn't assign credence to X, but he does assign credence to Y; and he also assigns credence to the proposition that sea level will rise by more than 2 cm in the next ten years, which we'll call Z. Here are their credences:

	X	Y	Z
Xia (C_1)	0.1	0.3	–
Yoaav (C_2)	–	0.5	0.4

How should we aggregate their credences? One easy option is to say that we should only aggregate their credences in the propositions to which they both assign credences. So, in this example, we aggregate their credences in Y only. That's possible for linear pooling: the aggregate is simply $1/20.3 + 1/20.5 = 0.4$. But it's not possible for geometric pooling: recall, in order to use that pooling strategy, you must have credences defined over a partition. In any case, it seems unsatisfactory to be left with only their pooled credences in one proposition. We'd like pooled credences in all three.

One proposal is an extension of the methods of minimal mutilation introduced in Section 5.1.3 and explored further in Section 7.1.[65] Here's the idea, which is due to Osherson & Vardi (2006): Fix a measure $\mathfrak{d}$ of the distance from one credence to another, and for credence functions C_1 and C_2 defined on $\mathscr{A}$, let $\mathfrak{D}(C_1, C_2) = \sum_{X \in \mathscr{A}} \mathfrak{d}(C_1(X), C_2(X))$. Then the pool of Xia's credences (C_1) and Yoaav's credences (C_2) is the probabilistic credence function P for which

---

[65] See Quintana (2024, Section 4.4) for an argument that this leads to using imprecise probabilities to pool precise probability functions.

the sum of the distance from P to C_1 and the distance from P to C_2 is minimal. More precisely, if $\mathscr{A}$ is the union of Xia's and Yoaav's agendas, so that $\mathscr{A} = \{X, Y, Z\}$:

$$\mathrm{CMM}_{\mathfrak{D}}(C_1, C_2) = \arg\min_{P \in \Delta_{\mathscr{A}}} (\mathfrak{d}(P(X), C_1(X)) + \mathfrak{d}(P(Y), C_1(Y))$$

$$+ \, \mathfrak{d}(P(Y), C_2(Y)) + \mathfrak{d}(P(Z), C_2(Z)))$$

In full generality, given credence functions $C_1, \ldots, C_n$ defined on $\mathscr{A}_1, \ldots, \mathscr{A}_n$ respectively, and letting $\mathscr{A} = \bigcup_{i=1}^{n} \mathscr{A}_i$,

$$\mathrm{CMM}_{\mathfrak{D}}(C_1, \ldots, C_n) = \arg\min_{P \in \Delta_{\mathscr{A}}} \sum_{i=1}^{n} \sum_{X \in \mathscr{A}_i} \mathfrak{d}(P(X), C_i(X))$$

Here are its outputs for squared Euclidean distance and generalized Kullback-Leibler:

	X	Y	Z
$\mathrm{CAP}_{\mathrm{SED}}(C_1, C_2)$	0.14	0.42	0.44
$\mathrm{CAP}_{\mathrm{GKL}}(C_1, C_2)$	0.116	0.418	0.466

But notice the following problem: X, Y, and Z form a partition. So, while Xia does not assign a credence to Z, the credences she assigns to X and Y do commit her to a credence in Z, namely the credence she must assign to Z if her credences are to be coherent: in her case, 0.6. And similarly, while Yoaav doesn't assign a credence to X, his credences in Y and Z commit him to assigning credence 0.1 to X. Now it seems natural to require of our pooling strategy for Xia and Yoaav that it should give the same result whether we pool their actual credences or their actual credences together with the credences to which their actual credences commit them. But the Principle of Coherent Minimal Mutilation does not do that. Their actual and committed credences and the results of applying that principle to them are given as follows.

	X	Y	Z
$\mathrm{Xia}^{\star}(C_1^{\star})$	0.1	0.3	0.6
$\mathrm{Yoaav}^{\star}(C_2^{\star})$	0.1	0.5	0.4
$\mathrm{CAP}_{\mathrm{SED}}(C_1^{\star}, C_2^{\star})$	0.1	0.4	0.5
$\mathrm{CAP}_{\mathrm{GKL}}(C_1^{\star}, C_2^{\star})$	0.102	0.396	0.502

That is, these two applications of the Principle of Coherent Minimal Mutilation violate what Pettigrew (2022) calls Extension Invariance:

Extension Invariance Suppose $P_1, \ldots, P_n$ are credence functions defined on $\mathscr{A}_1, \ldots, \mathscr{A}_n$. Then, if there are unique probabilistic credence functions

$P_1^\star, \ldots, P_n^\star$ defined on $\mathscr{A} = \bigcup_{i=1}^{n} \mathscr{A}_i$ such that $P_i^\star$ extends P_i, that is, $P_i^\star(X) = P_i(X)$ for all X in $\mathscr{A}_i$, then it should be that

$$F(P_1^\star, \ldots, P_n^\star) = F(P_1, \ldots, P_n)$$

Pettigrew (2022) considers a number of alternatives to the Principle of Coherent Minimal Mutilation and finds them all wanting except for the following, which he proposes:

> **Maximal Entropy Pooling** Pick a pooling strategy that applies to credence functions defined on the same agenda. Suppose $P_1, \ldots, P_n$ are defined on $\mathscr{A}_1, \ldots, \mathscr{A}_n$. Then, for each P_i, let $P_i^\star$ be the coherent extension of P_i to $\mathscr{A} = \bigcup_{i=1}^{n} \mathscr{A}_i$ that maximizes Shannon entropy. Then let
>
> $$\mathrm{ME}_F^*(P_1, \ldots, P_n) = F(P_1^\star, \ldots, P_n^\star)$$

This clearly satisfies Extension Invariance, since it deals with credence functions that have unique extensions. But it also gives plausible answers in other cases. For instance, suppose Zayn and Zara have the following credences:

	X	Y	Z
Zayn(C_1)	0.8	–	–
Zara(C_2)	–	–	0.8

Then here are the unique extensions with maximal entropy:

	X	Y	Z
Zayn*($C_1^\star$)	0.8	0.1	0.1
Zara*($C_2^\star$)	0.1	0.1	0.8

And here are the linear pools and geometric pools:

	X	Y	Z
$\mathrm{ME}_{\mathrm{LP}}(C_1^\star, C_2^\star)$	0.45	0.1	0.45
$\mathrm{ME}_{\mathrm{GP}}(C_1^\star, C_2^\star)$	0.425	0.15	0.425

8 Conclusion

The members of a group often disagree in their opinions about various matters. Nonetheless, we often need to identify a single set of opinions that resolves that disagreement and can stand for the group. We might want to summarize the opinions in the group, such as when we want to communicate succinctly the views of Shakespeare scholars concerning the authorship of *Hamlet*; or we might wish to identify the group's opinion in order to make a prediction ourselves or on their behalf, such as when we want to find the opinion of the climate science community concerning future sea level rise when we're debating the merits of different mitigation strategies; or we might need to ascribe opinions to the group treated as an agent in its own right in order to hold it accountable for certain collective actions its members have undertaken, as in the case of corporate responsibility.

Opinion pooling functions are tools we use for these purposes; and, as always with tools, different ones are apt for different purposes. We've enumerated many of the important features you might want a pooling strategy to have, and we've explained which ones have which features; and we've described certain sorts of goals you might have when you're pooling credences, and we've shown which pooling strategies best serve them. Perhaps the central insight of the Element is that, while the axiomatic approach to choosing between pooling strategies is powerful and has proved fruitful as means of characterizing different strategies, we often do better to look directly at the purpose for which we wish to use the pooling strategy and ask which will best serve that purpose. For instance, if our purpose is to arrive at accurate pooled credences, we should specify a measure of that accuracy and use that to evaluate the pooled credences given by different methods, without worrying about whether they satisfy the formal properties encoded in the axioms; if our purpose is to arrive at credences we can use to make decisions, then we look at the decisions licensed by the pooled credences that different strategies produce, again regardless of the axioms they satisfy; and similarly when we wish to use the pooled credences to judge whether a group is culpable when a decision they make causes undesirable consequences; and so on. If this is indeed the takeaway message, then no strategy does everything, but there are strategies that do a great deal and for each purpose there are strategies that serve it well. We hope that we have provided the guidance you might need to pick the one that will serve you best.

Appendix

Proof of Theorem 1

Theorem 1 (Madansky, 1964). *Suppose that*

(a) *P, Q are probabilistic credence functions defined on $\mathscr{A}$,*
(b) *$\Lambda = (\lambda, 1 - \lambda)$ is a sequence of weights,*
(c) *X and E are propositions in $\mathscr{A}$,*
(d) *$P(E), Q(E) > 0$,*

Then, if

$$\mathrm{LP}^\Lambda(P, Q)(X|E) = \mathrm{LP}^\Lambda(P(-|E), Q(-|E))(X)$$

Then at least one of the following must be true:

  (i) *Λ is dictatorial. That is, $\lambda = 0$ or $\lambda = 1$;*
 (ii) *$P(X|E) = Q(X|E)$; or*
(iii) *$P(E) = Q(E)$.*

Proof.

$$\mathrm{LP}^\Lambda(P, Q)(X|E) = \mathrm{LP}^\lambda(P(-|E), Q(-|E))(X)$$

iff

$$\frac{\lambda P(XE) + (1 - \lambda)Q(XE)}{\lambda P(E) + (1 - \lambda)Q(E)} = \lambda P(X|E) + (1 - \lambda)Q(X|E)$$

iff

$$\frac{\lambda(1 - \lambda)(Q(E) - P(E))(P(XE)Q(E) - Q(XE)P(E))}{P(E)Q(E)(\lambda P(E) + (1 - \lambda)Q(E))} = 0$$

iff

$$\lambda(1 - \lambda)(Q(E) - P(E))(P(XE)Q(E) - Q(XE)P(E)) = 0$$

iff at least one of the following is true:

  (i) $\lambda = 0$ or $\lambda = 1$;
 (ii) $P(X|E) = Q(X|E)$; or
(iii) $P(E) = Q(E)$.   □

Proof of Theorem 2

Theorem 2 (Laddaga, 1977; Lehrer & Wagner, 1983). *Suppose that*

(a) *P, Q are probabilistic credence functions defined on $\mathscr{A}$,*
(b) *$\Lambda = (\lambda, 1 - \lambda)$ is a sequence of weights,*
(c) *X and Y are propositions in $\mathscr{A}$.*

Then, if

(1) *P and Q both take X and Y to be independent – that is, $P(XY) = P(X)P(Y)$ and $Q(XY) = Q(X)Q(Y)$ – and*
(2) *$LP^{\Lambda}(P, Q)$ takes X and Y to be independent – that is, $LP^{\Lambda}(P, Q)(XY) = LP^{\Lambda}(P, Q)(X)LP^{\Lambda}(P, Q)(Y)$*

Then at least one of the following must be true:

(i) *Λ is dictatorial. That is, $\lambda = 0$ or $\lambda = 1$;*
(ii) *$P(X) = Q(X)$. That is, the individuals agree on how likely X is.*
(iii) *$P(Y) = Q(Y)$. That is, the individuals agree on how likely Y is.*

Proof.

$$LP^{\Lambda}(P, Q)(XY) = LP^{\Lambda}(P, Q)(X)LP^{\Lambda}(P, Q)(Y)$$

iff

$$\lambda P(X)P(Y) + (1 - \lambda)Q(X)Q(Y) = (\lambda P(X) + (1 - \lambda)Q(X))(\lambda P(Y) + (1 - \lambda)Q(Y))$$

iff

$$\lambda(1 - \lambda)(P(X) - Q(X))(P(Y) - Q(Y)) = 0$$

iff at least one of the following is true:

(i) Λ is dictatorial. That is, $\lambda = 0$ or $\lambda = 1$;
(ii) $P(X) = Q(X)$. That is, the individuals agree on how likely X is.
(iii) $P(Y) = Q(Y)$. That is, the individuals agree on how likely Y is.   □

Proof of Theorem 3

Theorem 3 (Aczél & Wagner, 1980; McConway, 1981). *If F is a pooling strategy defined for probability functions on an algebra over three or more worlds, and F satisfies Local Unanimity Preservation and Eventwise Independence, then there is a sequence of weights $\Lambda = (\lambda_1, \ldots, \lambda_n)$ such that, for any probabilistic credence functions $P_1, \ldots, P_n$,*

$$F(P_1, \ldots, P_n) = LP^{\Lambda}(P_1, \ldots, P_n)$$

Proof. Suppose F satisfies Local Unanimity Preservation and Eventwise Independence. That is,

(i) for all X, if $P_1(X) = \ldots = P_n(X)$, then

$$F(P_1, \ldots, P_n)(X) = P_1(X) = \ldots = P_n(X)$$

(ii) there is G such that, for all X,

$$F(P_1, \ldots, P_n)(X) = G(P_1(X), \ldots, P_n(X))$$

Now, pick X, Y, Z from $\mathscr{A}$ that partition the logical space. Now, pick real numbers $0 \leq a_1, \ldots, a_n, b_1, \ldots, b_n \leq 1$ with $a_i + b_i \leq 1$, for all $i = 1, \ldots, n$, and define $P_1, \ldots, P_n$ as follows:

$$P_i(X) = a_i \qquad P_i(Y) = b_i \qquad P_i(Z) = 1 - a_i - b_i$$

Then

$$F(P_1, \ldots, P_n)(X \vee Y) = F(P_1, \ldots, P_n)(X) + F(P_1, \ldots, P_n)(Y)$$

So, by Eventwise Independence,

$$G(a_1 + b_1, \ldots, a_n + b_n) = G(a_1, \ldots, a_n) + G(b_1, \ldots, b_n)$$

Now, for each $i = 1, \ldots, n$, define G_i as follows:

$$G_i(x) = G(\underbrace{0, \ldots, 0}_{i-1}, x, \underbrace{0, \ldots, 0}_{n-i})$$

Then

$$G(x_1, \ldots, x_n) = G_1(x_1) + \ldots + G_n(x_n)$$

and, for each $i = 1, \ldots, n$, and for all $0 \leq a, b \leq 1$ and $a + b \leq 1$,

$$G_i(a + b) = G_i(a) + G_i(b)$$

So G_i satisfies Cauchy's functional equation, and so there is λ_i such that $G_i(x) = \lambda_i x$ for all $0 \leq x \leq 1$. Since $G(x_1, \ldots, x_n)$ is always a probability, $\lambda_i \geq 0$. What's more, by Local Unanimity Preservation (i.e., (i) from the beginning of the proof),

$$1 = G(1, \ldots, 1) = G_1(1) + \ldots + G_n(1) = \lambda_1 + \ldots + \lambda_n$$

So $0 \leq \lambda_1, \ldots, \lambda_n \leq 1$ and $\lambda_1 + \ldots + \lambda_n = 1$ and

$$F(P_1, \ldots, P_n)(X) = G(P_1(X), \ldots, P_n(X)) =$$
$$G_1(P_1(X)) + \ldots + G_n(P_n(X)) = \lambda_1 P_1(X) + \ldots + \lambda_n P_n(X)$$

$\square$

Proof of Theorem 4

Theorem 4 (Raiffa, 1968). *Suppose that*

(a) *P, Q are probabilistic credence functions defined on $\mathscr{A}$,*
(b) *$\Lambda = (\lambda, 1 - \lambda)$ and $\Lambda' = (\lambda', 1 - \lambda')$ are sequences of weights,*
(c) *X and E are propositions in $\mathscr{A}$,*
(d) *$P(E), Q(E) > 0$,*

And suppose that

$$\mathrm{LP}^{\Lambda}(P, Q)(X|E) = \mathrm{LP}^{\Lambda'}(P(-|E), Q(-|E))(X)$$

Then

$$\lambda' = \frac{\lambda P(E)}{\lambda P(E) + (1 - \lambda)Q(E)}$$

and

$$1 - \lambda' = \frac{(1 - \lambda)Q(E)}{\lambda P(E) + (1 - \lambda)Q(E)}$$

Proof.

$$\mathrm{LP}^{\Lambda}(P, Q)(X|E) = \mathrm{LP}^{\Lambda'}(P(-|E), Q(-|E))(X)$$

iff

$$\frac{\lambda P(XE) + (1 - \lambda)Q(XE)}{\lambda P(E) + (1 - \lambda)Q(E)} = \lambda' P(X|E) + (1 - \lambda')Q(X|E)$$

iff

$$\lambda' = \frac{\lambda P(E)}{\lambda P(E) + (1 - \lambda)Q(E)} \qquad\qquad \square$$

Proof of Theorem 7

Theorem 7 (Pettigrew, 2019b). *Suppose $\mathfrak{I}$ is an additive and continuous inaccuracy measure. Then, if there is no sequence of weights $\Lambda = (\lambda_1, \ldots, \lambda_n)$ such that $Q = \mathrm{LP}^{\Lambda}(P_1, \ldots, P_n)$, then there is an alternative credence function $Q^{\star}$ such that, for each P_i,*

$$\mathbb{E}_{P_i}(\mathfrak{I}(Q^{\star})) = \sum_{X \in \mathscr{A}} P_i(w)\mathfrak{I}(Q^{\star}, w) < \sum_{X \in \mathscr{A}} P_i(w)\mathfrak{I}(Q, w) = \mathbb{E}_{P_i}(\mathfrak{I}(Q))$$

Proof. The proof proceeds in two stages. First, we use the additive and continuous inaccuracy measure $\mathfrak{I}$ to define a Bregman divergence $\mathfrak{D}$. Then we appeal to a result about Bregman divergences to establish the result.

Since $\Im$ is additive, there is $\mathfrak{s}$ such that

$$\Im(P, w) = \sum_{X \in \mathscr{A}} \mathfrak{s}(V_w(X), P(X))$$

Now define the divergence $\mathfrak{D}$ from P to P' as follows:

$$\mathfrak{D}(P, P') = \mathbb{E}_P(\Im(P')) - \mathbb{E}_P(\Im(P))$$

Then let $\varphi(p) = -p\mathfrak{s}(1, p) - (1 - p)\mathfrak{s}(0, p)$ and $\Phi(P) = \sum_{X \in \mathscr{A}} \varphi(P(X))$. Then it is possible to show that

$$\mathfrak{D}(P, P') = \Phi(P) - \Phi(P') - \nabla\Phi(P')(P - P')$$

So $\mathfrak{D}$ is a Bregman divergence.

Now we appeal to the following fact about Bregman divergences: if $\mathscr{X}$ is a set of credence functions and Q lies outside the convex hull $\mathscr{X}^+$ of $\mathscr{X}$, then there is $Q^\star$ in $\mathscr{X}^+$ such that, for all P in $\mathscr{X}$,

$$\mathfrak{D}(P, Q^\star) < \mathfrak{D}(P, Q)$$

So let $\mathscr{X} = \{P_1, \ldots, P_n\}$. Then if Q is not a linear pool of $P_1, \ldots, P_n$, then there is $Q^\star$ in $\mathscr{X}^+$ such that

$$\mathfrak{D}(P, Q^\star) < \mathfrak{D}(P, Q)$$

But then, by the definition of $\mathfrak{D}$,

$$\mathbb{E}_P(\Im(Q^\star)) - \mathbb{E}_P(\Im(P)) < \mathbb{E}_P(\Im(Q)) - \mathbb{E}_P(\Im(P))$$

So

$$\mathbb{E}_P(\Im(Q^\star)) < \mathbb{E}_P(\Im(Q))$$

as required. $\qquad\square$

Proof of Theorem 8

We state and prove a stronger version of the result, which is due to Pfau (2013). It holds for all Bregman divergences, not just squared Euclidean distance.

Theorem 8 (Pfau, 2013). *Suppose $\mathfrak{D}$ is a Bregman divergence. Suppose $(X_1, \ldots, X_m)$ is a sequence of quantities, whose true values are given by the sequence $T = (t_1, \ldots, t_m)$. For each individual i, $A_i = (a_{i1}, \ldots, a_{im})$ gives their estimates of the quantities. Then*

$$\mathfrak{D}\left(\frac{1}{n}\sum_{i=1}^{n} A_i, T\right) = \frac{1}{n}\sum_{i=1}^{n} \mathfrak{D}(A_i, T) - \frac{1}{n}\sum_{i=1}^{n} \mathfrak{D}\left(A_i, \frac{1}{n}\sum_{i=1}^{n} A_i\right)$$

Proof. Let $A^\star = \frac{1}{n} \sum_{i=1}^{n} A_i$. Now, since $\mathcal{D}$ is a Bregman divergence, there is Φ such that

$$\mathcal{D}(X,Y) = \Phi(X) - \Phi(Y) - \nabla\Phi(Y)(X-Y)$$

Then the result follows easily from the following three equations:

$$\mathcal{D}(A^\star, T) = \Phi(A^\star) - \Phi(T) - \nabla\Phi(T)(A^\star - T)$$

$$\frac{1}{n} \sum_{i=1}^{n} \mathcal{D}(A_i, T) = \frac{1}{n} \sum_{i=1}^{n} \left(\Phi(A_i) - \Phi(T) - \nabla\Phi(T) \left(\frac{1}{n} \sum_{i=1}^{n} A_i - T \right) \right)$$

$$= \frac{1}{n} \sum_{i=1}^{n} \left(\Phi(A_i) - \Phi(T) - \nabla\Phi(T) \left(A^\star - T \right) \right)$$

$$\frac{1}{n} \sum_{i=1}^{n} \mathcal{D}(A_i, A^\star) = \frac{1}{n} \sum_{i=1}^{n} \left(\Phi(A_i) - \Phi(A^\star) - \nabla\Phi(A^\star) \left(A_i - A^\star \right) \right)$$

$$= \frac{1}{n} \sum_{i=1}^{n} \left(\Phi(A_i) - \Phi(A^\star) \right) - \nabla\Phi(A^\star) \left(\frac{1}{n} \sum_{i=1}^{n} A_i - A^\star \right)$$

$$= \frac{1}{n} \sum_{i=1}^{n} \Phi(A_i) - \Phi(A^\star)$$

$$\square$$

Proof of Theorem 10

Theorem 10. *Suppose $X_1, \ldots, X_m$ is a sequence of quantities. For each individual i, $A_i = (a_{i1}, \ldots, a_{im})$ gives their estimates of the quantities. Now suppose that $A \neq \sum_{i=1}^{n} \frac{1}{n} A_i$. Then there are possible true values $T = (t_1, \ldots, t_m)$ of the quantities such that*

$$\mathrm{SED}\,(T,A) > \frac{1}{n} \sum_{i=1}^{n} \mathrm{SED}(T, A_i)$$

Proof. The right-hand side of the inequality is

$$\frac{1}{n} \sum_{i} \mathrm{SED}(T, A_i) = \frac{1}{n} \sum_{i} \sum_{j} (t_j - a_{ij})^2$$

$$= \frac{1}{n} \sum_{i} \sum_{j} \left(t_j^2 - 2a_{ij}t_j + a_{ji}^2 \right)$$

$$= \sum_{j} t_j^2 - 2\frac{1}{n} \sum_{i,j} a_{ij}t_j + \frac{1}{n} \sum_{i,j} a_{ij}^2$$

So $\text{SED}(T, A) > \frac{1}{n} \sum_i \text{SED}(T, A_i)$ iff

$$\sum_j a_j^2 - 2 \sum_j a_j t_j > \frac{1}{n} \sum_{i,j} a_{ij}^2 - 2 \sum_{i,j} \frac{1}{n} a_{ij} t_j$$

iff

$$2 \left(\sum_j \left(\frac{1}{n} \sum_i a_{ij} - a_j \right) t_j \right) > \frac{1}{n} \sum_{i,j} a_{ij}^2 - \sum_j a_j^2$$

And, if $(a_1, \ldots, a_n) \neq (\sum_i \frac{1}{n} a_{i1}, \ldots, \sum_i \frac{1}{n} a_{in})$, there is i such that $\sum_i \frac{1}{n} a_{ij} - a_j \neq 0$, and so it is always possible to choose $T = (t_1, \ldots, t_n)$ so that the inequality holds, as required. $\square$

Proof of Theorem 13

Theorem 13 (Mongin, 1995). *Suppose*

(a) *U is a utility function;*
(b) *F is a pooling strategy.*

If F is not a linear pooling strategy, then there are credence functions $P_1, \ldots, P_n$ and options A and B such that

(i) *$\mathbb{E}_{P_i}(U(A)) > \mathbb{E}_{P_i}(U(B))$, for each i, and*
(ii) *$\mathbb{E}_{F(P_1, \ldots, P_n)}(U(A)) < \mathbb{E}_{F(P_1, \ldots, P_n)}(U(B))$*

Proof. Given a probabilistic credence function P defined on an algebra generated by the partition $\mathcal{S} = \{S_1, \ldots, S_m\}$, represent P by the vector $\langle P(S_1), \ldots, P(S_m) \rangle$ in the m-dimensional unit cube $[0, 1]^m$. So, if $\mathcal{X}$ is a set of probabilistic credence functions on the algebra generated by $\mathcal{S}$, it is represented by a set of such vectors. Given a set $\mathcal{X}$ of such vectors, let $\mathcal{X}^+$ be the convex hull of $\mathcal{X}$: that is, $\mathcal{X}^+$ is the smallest convex set that contains $\mathcal{X}$; equivalently, if $\mathcal{X} = \{P_1, \ldots, P_n\}$,

$$\mathcal{X}^+ = \{\lambda_1 P_1 + \ldots + \lambda_n P_n : 0 \leq \lambda_1, \ldots, \lambda_n \leq 1\}$$

Now, suppose F is not a linear pooling strategy. Then there are credence functions $P_1, \ldots, P_n$ such that $F(P_1, \ldots, P_n)$ does not belong to $\{P_1, \ldots, P_n\}^+$. But now it follows from the Separating Hyperplane Theorem that there is a vector $A = \langle a_1, \ldots, a_m \rangle$ in $\mathbb{R}^m$ such that, for each P_i,

$$S \cdot P_i < S \cdot F(P_1, \ldots, P_n))$$

And therefore there is a real number b such that, for all P_i,

$$S \cdot P_i < b < S \cdot F(P_1, \ldots, P_n))$$

Then define the following two options:

(i) $U(A, S_j) = a_j$
(ii) $U(B, S_j) = b$

Then, for each P_i,

$$\mathbb{E}_{P_i}(U(A)) = \sum_{j=1}^{m} P_i(S_j)U(A, S_j) = S \cdot P_i < b = \mathbb{E}_{P_i}(U(B))$$

While

$$\mathbb{E}_{F(P_1,\ldots,P_n)}(U(A)) = \sum_{j=1}^{m} F(P_1,\ldots,P_n)(S_j)U(A, S_j)$$

$$= S \cdot F(P_1,\ldots,P_n) > b = \mathbb{E}_{F(P_1,\ldots,P_n)}(U(B)) \qquad \square$$

Proof That Linear Pooling Violates Deference Compatibility

Theorem (Dawid et al., 1995; Bradley, 2018; Gallow, 2018). *Suppose:*

(a) *X is a proposition;*
(b) *$\mathscr{A}$ is the random variable that give the credences that individual A assigns to X;*
(c) *$\mathscr{B}$ is the random variable that give the credences that individual B assigns to X;*
(d) *P is a credence function defined at least for conditional probabilities of the form $P(X|\mathscr{A} = a \ \& \ \mathscr{B} = b)$*

Then, if

 (i) *$P(\mathscr{A} = \mathscr{B}) < 1$;*
 (ii) *$P(X|\mathscr{A} = a) = a$, for all $0 \le a \le 1$;*
 (iii) *$P(X|\mathscr{B} = b) = b$, for all $0 \le b \le 1$;*
 (iv) *$P(X|\mathscr{A} = a \ \& \ \mathscr{B} = b) = \lambda a + (1 - \lambda)b$, for all $0 \le a, b \le 1$;*

then $\lambda = 0$ or $\lambda = 1$.

Proof. Our proof follows Gallow's. We suppose that (ii) and (iii) are true, and $0 < \lambda < 1$, and we derive the negation of (i).

First, we show that, for all $0 \le a, b \le 1$,

$$\mathbb{E}[\mathscr{A}|\mathscr{B} = b] = b \quad \text{and} \quad \mathbb{E}[\mathscr{B}|\mathscr{A} = a] = a$$

After all,

$$a = P(X|\mathscr{A} = a)$$

$$= \int_0^1 P(X|\mathscr{A} = a \ \& \ \mathscr{B} = b)P(\mathscr{B} = b|\mathscr{A} = a)\,db$$

$$= \int_0^1 (\lambda a + (1-\lambda)b)P(\mathscr{B} = b|\mathscr{A} = a)\,db$$

$$= \lambda a \int_0^1 P(\mathscr{B} = b|\mathscr{A} = a)\,db + (1-\lambda)\int_0^1 bP(\mathscr{B} = b|\mathscr{A} = a)\,db$$

$$= \lambda a + (1-\lambda)\mathbb{E}[\mathscr{B}|\mathscr{A} = a]$$

And so, if $0 < \lambda < 1$, then $\mathbb{E}[\mathscr{B}|\mathscr{A} = a] = a$. And similarly $\mathbb{E}[\mathscr{A}|\mathscr{B} = b] = b$.
Second, we use these identities to show that

$$\mathbb{E}[\mathscr{A}\mathscr{B}] = \mathbb{E}[\mathscr{A}^2] = \mathbb{E}[\mathscr{B}^2]$$

$$\mathbb{E}[\mathscr{A}\mathscr{B}] = \int_0^1 \int_0^1 abP(\mathscr{A} = a \ \& \ \mathscr{B} = b)\,db\,da$$

$$= \int_0^1 aP(\mathscr{A} = a)\left[\int_0^1 bP(\mathscr{B} = b|\mathscr{A} = a)\,db\right]da$$

$$= \int_0^1 aP(\mathscr{A} = a)\mathbb{E}[\mathscr{B}|\mathscr{A} = a]\,da$$

$$= \int_0^1 a^2 P(\mathscr{A} = a)\,da \quad \text{since } \mathbb{E}[\mathscr{B}|\mathscr{A} = a] = a$$

$$= \mathbb{E}[\mathscr{A}^2]$$

And similarly $\mathbb{E}[\mathscr{A}\mathscr{B}] = \mathbb{E}[\mathscr{B}^2]$.
Finally

$$\mathbb{E}[(\mathscr{A} - \mathscr{B})^2] = \mathbb{E}[\mathscr{A}^2] - 2\mathbb{E}[\mathscr{A}\mathscr{B}] + \mathbb{E}[\mathscr{B}^2] = 0$$

So $P(\mathscr{A} = \mathscr{B}) = 1$, which contradicts (i). $\qquad\qquad\square$

Proof That Multiplicative Pooling Satisfies Evidence Pooling

Theorem (Baccelli & Stewart, 2023). *Multiplicative pooling strategies satisfy Evidence Pooling.*

Proof. Suppose $\mathscr{S}$ is a partition and E is a disjunction of elements of that partition. Then first: suppose $S \in \mathscr{S}$ and $S \nsubseteq E_1 \ \& \ \dots \ \& \ E_n$. Then

$$\mathrm{MP}^{\Lambda}_{\mathscr{S}}(P_1,\dots,P_n)(S|E_1 \ \& \ \dots \ \& \ E_n) = 0 = \mathrm{MP}^{\Lambda}_{\mathscr{S}}(P_1(-|E_1),\dots,P_n(-|E_n))(S)$$

Now, second: suppose $S \subseteq E_1$ & $\ldots$ & E_n. Then

$$\text{MP}^{\Lambda}_{\mathscr{S}}(P_1(-|E_1), \ldots, P_n(-|E_n))(S) = \frac{\prod_{i=1}^{n} P_i(S|E_i)^{\lambda_i}}{\sum_{S' \in \mathscr{S}} \prod_{i=1}^{n} P_i(S'|E_i)^{\lambda_i}}$$

$$= \frac{\prod_{i=1}^{n} P_i(S|E_i)^{\lambda_i}}{\sum_{S' \subseteq E_1 \, \& \, \ldots \, \& \, E_n} \prod_{i=1}^{n} P_i(S'|E_i)^{\lambda_i}}$$

$$= \frac{\prod_{i=1}^{n} P_i(S)^{\lambda_i}}{\sum_{S' \subseteq E_1 \, \& \, \ldots \, \& \, E_n} \prod_{i=1}^{n} P_i(S')^{\lambda_i}}$$

$$= \text{MP}^{\Lambda}_{\mathscr{S}}(P_1, \ldots, P_n)(S|E_1 \, \& \, \ldots \, \& \, E_n)$$

$\square$

Inaccuracy Measures

An *inaccuracy measure* is a function $\mathfrak{I}$ that takes a credence function P and a world w and returns the inaccuracy $\mathfrak{I}(P, w)$ of P at w.

- $\mathfrak{I}$ is *additive* if there is a function $\mathfrak{s} : [0, 1] \to [0, \infty]$ such that

$$\mathfrak{I}(P, w) = \sum_{X \in \mathscr{A}} \mathfrak{s}(V_w(X), P(X))$$

In this case, we think of $\mathfrak{s}(1, p)$ as the inaccuracy of credence p in a true proposition and $\mathfrak{s}(0, p)$ as the inaccuracy of a credence p in a falsehood. We call $\mathfrak{s}$ a *scoring rule*.
- $\mathfrak{s}$ is *continuous* if $\mathfrak{s}(1, x)$ and $\mathfrak{s}(0, x)$ are continuous functions of x.
- $\mathfrak{s}$ is strictly proper if for any $0 \leq p \leq 1$,

$$p\mathfrak{s}(1, x) + (1 - p)\mathfrak{s}(0, x)$$

is minimized, as a function of x, at $x = p$. That is, each probability expects itself to be most accurate.

References

Aczél, J., & Wagner, C. G. (1980). A characterization of weighted arithmetic means. *SIAM Journal on Algebraic Discrete Methods*, *1*(3), 259–260.

Akerlof, G. (1970). The market for "lemons": Quality, uncertainty, the market mechanism. *The Quarterly Journal of Economics*, *84*(3), 488–500.

Arntzenius, F. (2008). No regrets, or: Edith piaf revamps decision theory. *Erkenntnis*, *68*, 277–297.

Arrow, K. J. (1951). *Social Choice and Individual Values*. New York: Wiley.

Arvan, M. (2020). *Neurofunctional Prudence and Morality: A Philosophical Theory*. Routledge.

Baccelli, J., & Stewart, R. T. (2023). Support for geometric pooling. *The Review of Symbolic Logic*, *16*(1), 298–337.

Baron, J., Mellers, B. A., Tetlock, P. E., Stone, E., & Ungar, L. H. (2014). Two reasons to make aggregated probability forecasts more extreme. *Decision Analysis*, *11*(2), 133–145.

Basu, R. (2019). Radical moral encroachment: The moral stakes of racist beliefs. *Philosophical Issues*, *29*(1), 9–23.

Bazargan-Forward, S. (2017). Complicity. In M. Jankovic, & K. Ludwig (Eds.) *Routledge Handbook on Collective Intentionality*, (pp. 327–337). London: Routledge.

Benjamin, D. J., Berger, J. O., Johannesson, M., et al. (2018). Redefine statistical significance. *Nature Human Behaviour*, *2*(1), 6–10.

Bovens, L., & Hartmann, S. (2004). *Bayesian Epistemology*. Oxford: Oxford University Press.

Bradley, R. (2018). Learning from others: Conditioning versus averaging. *Theory and Decision*, *85*(1), 5–20.

Bradley, S. (2016). Imprecise probabilities. In E. N. Zalta (Ed.) *Stanford Encyclopedia of Philosophy*. Metaphysics Research Lab, Stanford University.

Briggs, R. A., & Pettigrew, R. (2020). An accuracy-dominance argument for conditionalization. *Noûs*, *54*(1), 162–181.

Christensen, D. (2007). Epistemology of disagreement: The good news. *The Philosophical Review*, *116*(2), 187–217.

Christensen, D. (2009). Disagreement as evidence: The epistemology of controversy. *Philosophy Compass*, *4*(5), 756–767.

Couso, I., & Moral, S. (2011). Sets of desirable gambles: Conditioning, representation, and precise probabilities. *International Journal of Approximate Reasoning*, *52*(7), 1034–1055.

Cozman, F. G. (2012). Sets of probability distributions, independence, and convexity. *Synthese, 186*, 577–600.

D'Agostino, M., & Sinigaglia, C. (2010). Epistemic accuracy and subjective probability. In M. Suárez, M. Dorato, & M. Rédei (Eds.) *EPSA Epistemology and Methodology of Science: Launch of the European Philosophy of Science Association*, (pp. 95–105). Netherlands: Springer.

Dawid, P., DeGroot, M. H., Mortera, J., et al. (1995). Coherent combination of experts' opinions. *Test, 4*(2), 263–313.

Dawid, P., & Mortera, J. (2020). Resolving some contradictions in the theory of linear opinion pools. *Theory and Decision, 88*, 453–456.

de Condorcet, N. (1785). *Essay sur l'Application de l'Analyse à la Probabilité des Décisions Rendue à la Pluralité des Voix*. Paris.

de Finetti, B. (1974). *Theory of Probability*, vol. 1. New York: Wiley.

DeGroot, M. H. (1974). Reaching a consensus. *Journal of the American Statistical Association, 69*(345), 118–121.

Dietrich, F. (2010). Bayesian group belief. *Social Choice and Welfare, 35*(4), 595–626.

Dietrich, F., & List, C. (2015). Probabilistic opinion pooling. In A. Hájek, & C. R. Hitchcock (Eds.) *Oxford Handbook of Philosophy and Probability* (pp. 519–542). Oxford: Oxford University Press.

Dietrich, F., & List, C. (2017). Probabilistic opinion pooling generalized. Part one: General agendas. *Social Choice and Welfare, 48*, 747–786.

Dogramaci, S., & Horowitz, S. (2016). An argument for uniqueness about evidential support. *Philosophical Issues, 26*(1), 130–147.

Dubois, D., & Prade, H. (1988). *Possibility Theory: An Approach to Computerized Processing of Uncertainty*. New York: Plenum Press.

Easwaran, K., Fenton-Glynn, L., Hitchcock, C., & Velasco, J. D. (2016). Updating on the credences of others: Disagreement, agreement, and synergy. *Philosophers' Imprint, 16*(11), 1–39.

Ebner, L., Schwaferts, P. M., & Augustin, T. (2019). Robust Bayes factor for independent two-sample comparisons under imprecise prior information. In *International Symposium on Imprecise Probabilities: Theories and Applications*, (pp. 167–174). PMLR.

Elga, A. (2007). Reflection and disagreement. *Noûs, 41*(3), 478–502.

Elkin, L. (2021). Regret averse opinion aggregation. *Ergo an Open Access Journal of Philosophy, 8*(16), 473–495.

Elkin, L. (2023). The precautionary principle and expert disagreement. *Erkenntnis, 88*(6), 2717–2726.

Elkin, L., & Wheeler, G. (2018). Resolving peer disagreements through imprecise probabilities. *Noûs, 52*(2), 260–278.

Feldman, R. (2006). Reasonable religious disagreements. In L. Antony (Ed.) *Philosophers without Gods: Meditations on Atheism and the Secular Life* (pp. 194–214). Oxford: Oxford University Press.

Fitelson, B. (1999). The plurality of Bayesian measures of confirmation and the problem of measure sensitivity. *Philosophy of Science, 66*(S3), S362–S378.

Gallow, J. D. (2018). No one can serve two epistemic masters. *Philosophical Studies, 175*(10), 2389–2398.

Galton, F. (1907). Vox Populi. *Nature, 75,* 450–451.

Genest, C. (1984). A characterization theorem for externally Bayesian groups. *Annals of Statistics, 12*(3), 1100–1105.

Genest, C., Weerahandi, S., & Zidek, J. V. (1984). Aggregating opinions through logarithmic pooling. *Theory and Decision, 17*(1), 61.

Genest, C., & Zidek, J. V. (1986). Combining probability distributions: A critique and an annotated bibliography. *Statistical Science, 1*(1), 114–135.

Gilbert, M. (2006). Rationality in collective action. *Philosophy of the Social Sciences, 36*(1), 3–17.

Gilbert, M. (2013). *Joint Commitment: How We Make the Social World.* Oxford: Oxford University Press.

Gilboa, I., & Schmeidler, D. (1989). Maxmin expected utility with non-unique prior. *Journal of Mathematical Economics, 18*(2), 141–153.

Goldman, A. I. (2014). Social process reliabilism. In J. Lackey (Ed.) *Essays in Collective Epistemology,* (pp. 13–41). Oxford: Oxford University Press.

Greaves, H., & Wallace, D. (2006). Justifying conditionalization: Conditionalization maximizes expected epistemic utility. *Mind, 115*(459), 607–632.

Hakli, R. (2011). On dialectical justification of group beliefs. In H. B. Schmid, D. Sirtes, & M. Weber (Eds.) *Collective Epistemology,* (pp. 119–153). Berlin: Ontos Verlag.

Hegselmann, R., & Krause, U. (2002). Opinion dynamics and bounded confidence models, analysis and simulation. *Journal of Artificial Societies and Social Simulation, 5*(3) 1–33.

Hild, M. (2001). Stable aggregation of preferences. *Social Science Working Paper* 1112. California Institute of Technology.

Huemer, M. (2011). Epistemological egoism and agent-centered norms. In T. Dougherty (Ed.) *Evidentialism and Its Discontents,* (p. 17). Oxford: Oxford University Press.

Jehle, D., & Fitelson, B. (2009). What is the "equal weight view"? *Episteme, 6*(3), 280–293.

Jorgensen Bolinger, R. (2020). Varieties of moral encroachment. *Philosophical Perspectives, 34*(1), 5–26.

Joyce, J. M. (1998). A nonpragmatic vindication of probabilism. *Philosophy of Science, 65*(4), 575–603.

Joyce, J. M. (1999). *The Foundations of Causal Decision Theory*. Cambridge Studies in Probability, Induction, and Decision Theory. Cambridge: Cambridge University Press.

Joyce, J. M. (2009). Accuracy and coherence: Prospects for an alethic epistemology of partial belief. In F. Huber, & C. Schmidt-Petri (Eds.) *Degrees of Belief* (pp. 263–297). London: Springer.

Joyce, J. M. (2010). A defense of imprecise credences in inference and decision making. *Philosophical Perspectives, 24,* 281–322.

Kelly, T. (2005). The epistemic significance of disagreement. In J. Hawthorne, & T. G. Szabo (Eds.) *Oxford Studies in Epistemology*, vol. 1, (pp. 167–196). Oxford University Press.

Kelly, T. (2011). Peer disagreement and higher order evidence. In A. Goldman, & D. Whitcomb (Eds.) *Social Epistemology: Essential Readings*, (pp. 183–217). Oxford: Oxford University Press.

King, N. L. (2012). Disagreement: What's the problem? Or a good peer is hard to find. *Philosophy and Phenomenological Research, 85*(2), 249–272.

Konek, J. (2019). *IP Scoring Rules: Foundations and Applications*. Proceedings of the Eleventh International Symposium on Imprecise Probabilities: Theories and Applications, vol. 103, (pp. 256–264).

Konieczny, S., & Pino Pérez, R. (1998). On the logic of merging. In *Proceedings of KR'98*, (pp. 488–498).

Konieczny, S., & Pino Pérez, R. (1999). Merging with integrity constraints. In *Fifth European Conference on Symbolic and Quantitative Approaches to Reasoning with Uncertainty (ECSQARU'99)*, (pp. 233–244).

Kopec, M. (2019). Unifying group rationality. *Ergo: An Open Access Journal of Philosophy, 6,* 517–544.

Kornhauser, L. A., & Sager, L. G. (1986). Unpacking the court. *Yale Law Journal, 96,* 82–117.

Kutz, C. (2000). *Complicity: Ethics and Law for a Collective Age*. New York: Cambridge University Press.

Kyburg, H. E. (1961). *Probability and the Logic of Rational Belief*. Middletown: Wesleyan University Press.

Kyburg, H. E., & Pittarelli, M. (1996). Set-based Bayesianism. *IEEE Transactions on Systems, Man, and Cybernetics-Part A: Systems and Humans, 26*(3), 324–339.

Lackey, J. (2010). A justificationist view of disagreement's epistemic significance. In A. Haddock, A. Millar, & D. Pritchard (Eds.) *Social Epistemology* (pp. 145–154). Oxford: Oxford University Press.

Lackey, J. (2016). What is justified group belief? *Philosophical Review, 125*(3), 341–396.

Laddaga, R. (1977). Lehrer and the consensus proposal. *Synthese, 36*, 473–477.

Lehrer, K. (1976). When rational disagreement is impossible. *Noûs, 10*, 327–332.

Lehrer, K., & Wagner, C. (1983). Probability amalgamation and the independence issue: A reply to Laddaga. *Synthese, 55*(3), 339–346.

Leitgeb, H., & Pettigrew, R. (2010a). An objective justification of Bayesianism I: Measuring inaccuracy. *Philosophy of Science, 77*, 201–235.

Leitgeb, H., & Pettigrew, R. (2010b). An objective justification of Bayesianism II: The consequences of minimizing inaccuracy. *Philosophy of Science, 77*, 236–272.

Levi, I. (1974). On indeterminate probabilities. *Journal of Philosophy, 71*, 391–418.

Levi, I. (1985). Consensus as shared agreement and outcome of inquiry. *Synthese, 62*(1), 3–11.

Levinstein, B. A. (2017). Permissive rationality and sensitivity. *Philosophy and Phenomenological Research, 94*(2), 342–370.

Lewis, D. (1999). Why conditionalize? In *Papers in Metaphysics and Epistemology*, (pp. 403–407). Cambridge: Cambridge University Press.

List, C., & Pettit, P. (2002). Aggregating sets of judgments: An impossibility result. *Economics & Philosophy, 18*(1), 89–110.

List, C., & Pettit, P. (2011). *Group Agency: The Possibility, Design, and Status of Corporate Agents*. Oxford: Oxford University Press.

Loomes, G., & Sugden, R. (1982). Regret theory: An alternative theory of rational choice under uncertainty. *The Economic Journal, 92*(368), 805–824.

Madansky, A. (1964). Externally Bayesian groups. Memorandum rm-4141-pr, The RAND Corporation. www.rand.org/content/dam/rand/pubs/research _memoranda/2008/RM4141.pdf.

Mayo-Wilson, C. & Wheeler, G. (2016). Scoring Imprecise Credences: A Mildly Immodest Proposal. *Philosophy and Phenomenological Research, 93*(1), 55–78.

Makinson, D. (1965). The paradox of the preface. *Analysis, 25*(6), 205–207.

Matheson, J., & Frances, B. (2018). Disagreement. In E. N. Zalta (Ed.) *Stanford Encyclopedia of Philosophy*. Metaphysics Research Lab, Stanford University.

McConway, K. J. (1981). Marginalization and linear opinion pools. *Journal of the American Statistical Association, 76*, 410–414.

Mongin, P. (1995). Consistent Bayesian aggregation. *Journal of Economic Theory, 66*(2), 313–351.

Morris, P. A. (1983). An axiomatic approach to expert resolution. *Management Science, 29*(1), 24–32.

Moss, S. (2011). Scoring rules and epistemic compromise. *Mind, 120*(480), 1053–1069.

Moss, S. (2018). Moral encroachment. *Proceedings of the Aristotelian Society, 118*(2), 177–205.

Nau, R. F. (2002). The aggregation of imprecise probabilities. *Journal of Statistical Planning and Inference, 105*(1), 265–282.

Nielsen, M. (2021). Accuracy-dominance and conditionalization. *Philosophical Studies, 178*(10), 1–20.

Osherson, D., & Vardi, M. Y. (2006). Aggregating disparate estimates of chance. *Games and Economical Behavior, 56*(1), 148–173.

Page, S. E. (2007). *The Difference: How the Power of Diversity Creates Better Groups, Firms, Schools, and Societies*. Princeton: Princeton University Press.

Pettigrew, R. (2016). *Accuracy and the Laws of Credence*. Oxford: Oxford University Press.

Pettigrew, R. (2019a). Aggregating incoherent agents who disagree. *Synthese, 196*, 2737–2776.

Pettigrew, R. (2019b). On the accuracy of group credences. In T. S. Gendler, & J. Hawthorne (Eds.) *Oxford Studies in Epistemology*, vol. 6, (pp. 137–160). Oxford: Oxford University Press.

Pettigrew, R. (2022). Aggregating agents with opinions about different propositions. *Synthese, 200*(5), 1–25.

Pfau, D. (2013). A Generalized Bias-Variance Decomposition for Bregman Divergences. http://davidpfau.com/assets/generalized_bvd_proof.pdf.

Pigozzi, G. (2006). Belief merging and the discursive dilemma: An argument-based approach to paradoxes of judgment aggregation. *Synthese, 152*, 285–298.

Predd, J., Seiringer, R., Lieb, E. H., et al. (2009). Probabilistic coherence and proper scoring rules. *IEEE Transactions of Information Theory, 55*(10), 4786–4792.

Predd, J. B., Osherson, D., Kulkarni, S., & Poor, H. V. (2008). Aggregating probabilistic forecasts from incoherent and abstaining experts. *Decision Analysis, 5*(4), 177–189.

Quintana, I. O. (2024). Radical pooling and imprecise probabilities. *Erkenntnis, 89*, 153–180.

Raiffa, H. (1968). *Decision Analysis: Introductory Lectures on Choices under Uncertainty*. Reading: Addison-Wesley.

Ramsey, F. P. (1926 [1931]). Truth and probability. In R. B. Braithwaite (Ed.) *The Foundations of Mathematics and Other Logical Essays*, chap. VII, (pp. 156–198). London: Kegan, Paul, Trench, Trubner.

Ranjan, R., & Gneiting, T. (2010). Combining probability forecasts. *Journal of the Royal Statistical Society Series B: Statistical Methodology, 72*(1), 71–91.

Rosen, G. (2001). Nominalism, naturalism, and epistemic relativism. *Philosophical Perspectives, 15,* 69–91.

Satopää, V. A., Baron, J., Foster, D. P., et al. (2014). Combining multiple probability predictions using a simple logit model. *International Journal of Forecasting, 30*(2), 344–356.

Savage, L. J. (1954). *The Foundations of Statistics*. New York: John Wiley & Sons.

Savage, L. J. (1971). Elicitation of personal probabilities and expectations. *Journal of the American Statistical Association, 66*(336), 783–801.

Schmitt, F. F. (1994). The justification of group beliefs. In F. F. Schmitt (Ed.) *Socializing Epistemology: The Social Dimensions of Knowledge*, (pp. 257–287). London: Rowman and Littlefield.

Schoenfield, M. (2017). The Accuracy and Rationality for Imprecise Credences. *Noûs, 51*(4), 667–685.

Seidenfeld, T. (2004). A contrast between two decision rules for use with (convex) sets of probabilities: Gamma-maximin versus E-admissibility. *Synthese, 140,* 69–88.

Seidenfeld, T., Kadane, J. B., & Schervish, M. J. (1989). On the shared preferences of two Bayesian decision makers. *The Journal of Philosophy, 86*(5), 225–244.

Seidenfeld, T., J. Schervish, M. J. & Kadane, J. B. (2012). Forecasting with imprecise probabilities. *International Journal of Approximate Reasoning, 53,* 1248–1261.

Shafer, G. (1976). *A Mathematical Theory of Evidence*. Princeton: Princeton University Press.

Soll, J. B., & Larrick, R. P. (2009). Strategies for revising judgment: How (and how well) people use others' opinions. *Journal of Experimental Psychology: Learning, Memory, and Cognition, 35*(3), 780.

Stewart, R. T., & Quintana, I. O. (2018). Probabilistic opinion pooling with imprecise probabilities. *Journal of Philosophical Logic, 47,* 17–45.

Stone, M. (1961). The opinion pool. *The Annals of Mathematical Statistics, 32*(4), 1339–1342.

Titelbaum, M. G. (2015). Rationality's fixed point (Or: In defense of right reason). In J. Hawthorne, & T. S. Gendler (Eds.) *Oxford Studies in Epistemology*, vol. 5, (pp. 253–294). Oxford: Oxford University Press.

Tuomela, R. (1992). Group beliefs. *Synthese, 91*(3), 285–318.

Tuomela, R., & Mäkelä, P. (2016). Group agents and their responsibility. *The Journal of Ethics, 20*(1), 299–316.

van Inwagen, P. (1996). It is wrong, always, everywhere, and for anyone, to believe anything, upon insufficient evidence. In J. Jordan, & D. Howard-Snyder (Eds.) *Faith, Freedom, and Rationality,* (pp. 137–154). Hanham: Rowman and Littlefield.

Vicig, P., & Seidenfeld, T. (2012). Bruno de finetti and imprecision: Imprecise probability does not exist! *International Journal of Approximate Reasoning, 53*(8), 1115–1123.

Wagner, C. (1978). Consensus through respect: A model of rational group decision-making. *Philosophical Studies: An International Journal for Philosophy in the Analytic Tradition, 34*(4), 335–349.

Wagner, C. (2010). Jeffrey conditioning and external Bayesianity. *Logic Journal of IGPL, 18*(2), 336–345.

Walley, P. (1982). The elicitation and aggregation of beliefs. *Technical Report 23.*

Walley, P. (1991). *Statistical Reasoning with Imprecise Probabilities,* vol. 42 of *Monographs on Statistics and Applied Probability.* London: Chapman and Hall.

Wedgwood, R. (2007). *The Nature of Normativity.* Oxford: Oxford University Press.

Weirich, P. (2020). Causal decision theory. In E. N. Zalta (Ed.) *The Stanford Encyclopedia of Philosophy.* Metaphysics Research Lab, Stanford University.

Weirich, P. (2021). *Rational Choice Using Imprecise Probabilities and Utilities.* Elements in Decision Theory and Philosophy. Cambridge: Cambridge University Press.

Weisberg, J., & Pettigrew, R. (2023). Geometric pooling: A user's guide. *The British Journal for the Philosophy of Science.* www.journals.uchicago.edu/doi/10.1086/727000.

Winkler, R. L. (1968). The consensus of subjective probability distributions. *Management Science, 15*(2), B61–B75.

Zhang, S. (ms). Coherent combination of Experts' Opinions: Another impossibility result.

Acknowledgments

We are grateful for the feedback provided by Frederik Van De Putte, Erica Yu, Mans Abrahamson, and two anonymous reviewers on earlier manuscripts. Lee Elkin was supported by the Dutch Research Council (NWO) through the ENCODE Vidi project (VI.Vidi.191.105). Richard Pettigrew was supported by a British Academy Mid-Career Fellowship (MF21\210022). Work on this Element was facilitated by research visits at the University of Bristol (Lee Elkin, fall 2023) and Erasmus University Rotterdam (Richard Pettigrew, winter 2023), both funded by the ENCODE project.

Cambridge Elements ≡

Decision Theory and Philosophy

Martin Peterson
Texas A&M University

Martin Peterson is Professor of Philosophy and Sue and Harry E. Bovay Professor of the History and Ethics of Professional Engineering at Texas A&M University. He is the author of four books and one edited collection, as well as many articles on decision theory, ethics and philosophy of science.

About the Series

This Cambridge Elements series offers an extensive overview of decision theory in its many and varied forms. Distinguished authors provide an up-to-date summary of the results of current research in their fields and give their own take on what they believe are the most significant debates influencing research, drawing original conclusions.

Cambridge Elements ≡

Decision Theory and Philosophy

Elements in the Series

A full series listing is available at: www.cambridge.org/EDTP